Reflective Reflections

The new comprehensive book on eating disorders

Katy Sara Culling

chipmunkapublishing
the mental health publisher

Reflective Reflections

All rights reserved, no part of this publication may be reproduced by any means, electronic, mechanical photocopying, documentary, film or in any other format without prior written permission of the publisher.

Published by
Chipmunkapublishing
PO Box 6872
Brentwood
Essex CM13 1ZT
United Kingdom

http://www.chipmunkapublishing.com

Copyright © Katy Sara Culling 2010

Chipmunkapublishing gratefully acknowledge the support of Arts Council England.

Previous works by Katy Sara Culling:

DARK CLOUDS GATHER: The true story about surviving Mood Disorders, Eating Disorders, Attempted Suicide and Self Harm.

TOO GOOD FOR THIS WORLD: True Stories from People with Mood Disorders.

Reflective Reflections

Katy Sara Culling

Dedicated to my Psychotherapist at Cotswold House,
The Oxford Adult Eating Disorder Service.
Who taught me I was not a chicken.

Reflective Reflections

Author Biography

Katy Sara Culling was born in Liverpool, North England, in January 1975, sharing her birth date rather aptly with Virginia Woolf. Daughter of Sue and Paul Culling, her family moved back to its roots in Derbyshire, where she grew up along with her younger sister Beth, in the village of Castle Donington, on the Derbyshire-Leicestershire border. However, even as young as 5 she exhibited symptoms of bipolar disorder. She attended a private school for girls, Loughborough High School, where she was a high achieving student. Unfortunately, due to bullying and also to numb her mania and depression, she developed anorexia nervosa and began to self-harm.

Katy Sara then went to The University of Nottingham, where she studied Biochemistry and Nutrition. She did her (1st class) thesis on alcohol and metabolism, interested in the psychology of Alcoholism. All this was done despite considerable illness including over 60 suicide attempts and purging-type anorexia – and yet more bullying. Her good work at Nottingham lead to an offer of a place at The University of Oxford, where she studied for a PhD (DPhil) in Clinical Medicine. In her final year she became so ill with anorexia that she was in hospital (first as a day patient, then an inpatient, and eventually a sectioned inpatient). During those two years she attempted suicide over 300 times, dying twice, only to be revived. She finally, at the age of 28 got a diagnosis of bipolar disorder and the correct medication, and had been mostly fine ever since. Her eating disorder spontaneously recovered. She later wrote up her PhD thesis and published her results.

Now Katy Sara is mostly well and has become a writer, wanting to prevent others from suffering as she did. She

Reflective Reflections

writes mainly about bipolar disorder and anorexia but also other psychiatry/mental health topics, and her first anorexia/bipolar memoir Dark Clouds Gather (autobiographical) was published by Chipmunkapublishing.

Her second book, Too Good For This World, a collection of stories from people with bipolar disorder and major depression is also available, including people with eating disorders. Katy Sara also spends her time working in medical research, and helping fellow survivors of anorexia, bulimia and bipolar disorder through charitable organisations whilst trying to maintain her own good mental health. She is an advocate for all survivors of these illnesses and believes that an "expert patient" system could be highly beneficial. She has not ruled out the possibility of doing another PhD, this time in Psychiatry. Every day is a battle with illness that she wins, and she hopes that 443 suicide attempts will never reach 444 and that her battle with food remains one that she feels she has won.

Acknowledgements

The Oxford Adult Eating Disorder Service who taught me a lot of the good things I needed to know to battle my anorexia, in particular my individual psychotherapist.

Paula Radcliffe for taking time out of her busy schedule to write a comment in this book.

My family for living with me whilst I was ill: a bitch or worse, and particularly when you all knew I was bingeing and purging leaving an awful mess and wasting so much money on food that would never be digested. I know now that it really affected you all deeply.

Thank you to my GP Dr Carol McGrath for all she did to treat and support me through one of the most difficult times of my life – fighting my purging-type anorexia.

Thank you to Nottingham and Oxford universities for allowing me time out for treatment.

For all the patients and staff who went through day hospital treatment with me at Leicester and at Oxford – sorry for being such a difficult patient and a special thank you to those who have kept in touch with me: Clare, J, Julius, Becky, Ayeesha and Rose.

Sarah Mercer for proof reading and for telling her story of having Binge Eating Disorder.
Lynne Moore for sharing her story of anorexia with us.

Front Cover Illustration by Mike Kerins

Reflective Reflections

INDEX

Acknowledgements

INTRODUCTION: Seductive control that is not control.

Chapter 1: Anorexia Nervosa.

- ❖ List of Diagnostic Symptoms of Anorexia Nervosa
- o Predisposing, precipitating and maintaining factors
- o Delving a little deeper into the behaviours in Anorexia Nervosa: warning signs
- ♦ Expert Opinion by Paula Radcliffe, Sports Personality and World Record Marathon Holder
- o Treatments for Anorexia Nervosa
- o Final Thought on Anorexia and Image

Chapter 2: Bulimia Nervosa.

- ❖ List of Diagnostic Symptoms of Bulimia Nervosa
- ♠ Figure 1: The vicious circle of non-control in Bulimia Nervosa (and Anorectic Bulimia)
- o Predisposing, precipitating and maintaining factors
- o Delving a little deeper into the behaviours in Bulimia Nervosa: warning signs

Reflective Reflections

   o   Treatments for Bulimia Nervosa

Chapter 3: E.D.N.O.S. Eating Disorder Not Otherwise Specified.

❖ List of Diagnostic Symptoms of E.D.N.O.S.

Chapter 4: Compulsive Over Eating and Binge Eating Disorder.

♠ Figure 2: The vicious circle of feelings and bingeing in B.E.D

Chapter 5: Thinking Cap On With Respect To Eating Disorders.

♠ Figure 3: Questionable Anorexia-Bulimia Spectrum

♠ Figure 4: Normal, Borderline Disordered and Disordered Eating represented Diagrammatically

Chapter 6: Complex Needs.

   o   Mood Disorders in Eating Disorders

♠ Figure 5: Prevalence of Depression (type unspecified) in people with Different Eating Disorders

♠ Figure 6: Prevalence of Recognised and Unrecognised Depression (type unspecified) in people with Eating Disorders of all types

   o   Dependency issues

- Diabetes

- Pregnancy

- Myalgic Encephalopathy/Encephalomyelitis (M.E.), also known as Chronic Fatigue Syndrome (C.F.S)

- Irritable Bowel Syndrome, (I.B.S)

Chapter 7: Eating Disorders: some tips from sufferers to carers and professionals.

Chapter 8: Less well known and Unofficial Eating Disorders, Similar Illnesses and Behaviours.

Chapter 9: Eating Disorders and the Dangers of the Internet.

Chapter 10: A survivor and a non-survivor personal experience of Anorexia, a survivor experience of Bulimia and a survivor experience of B.E.D.

Chapter 11: Hope.

Useful websites and books.

Reflective Reflections

INTRODUCTION: Seductive control that is *not* control.

> "Bone and Skin, two millers thin,
> Would starve us all, or near it;
> But be it known to Skin and Bone
> That Flesh and Blood can't bear it."
>
> ❧ John Byrom of Manchester (1692 - 1763).
> English poet, hymnist, and inventor of a system of shorthand

In our Western world of plenty, the constraining, tangible corsets of days-gone-by have been replaced by a new, metaphorical corset of the mind. Men and women, all of whom suffer from extreme low self-esteem and lack of validation, find themselves living out each day of their life, overwhelmed with issues of food, weight, size, self-hatred, illness, anxiety, anger, guilt, control and fear. Eating disorders are a *symptom* of deep emotional distress, which entrap sufferers and create new problems of their own. Societally, dieting is rife. Value judgements based on a person's size are copious, and seemingly up for discussion without any understanding of any possible underlying issues. Few illnesses inspire such misunderstanding, despair and frustration, (for *all* involved), as do eating disorders. Few illnesses are awarded such warped attention in the media; or are claimed to be "lifestyle choices" by some of those afflicted.

Statistics on eating disorders do not inspire confidence because of the very secret nature of these illnesses (and varying diagnostic criteria used). The UK based

Reflective Reflections

"Beat," formerly the Eating Disorders Association, believes that the number of people actually *receiving treatment* for anorexia or bulimia in the UK is near to 90,000 (much higher than the official figure). Many, many more people receive no help and no diagnosis, in particular those with bulimia (it is believed, because the sufferer feels particularly ashamed of their actions whereas an anorectic is proud of her or his weight loss). The organisation "Beat" estimates that 1.1 *million* people in the UK are afflicted by anorexia or bulimia.[1]

According to the National Institute of Mental Health in America, 5-10 million US citizens have eating disorders, including anorexia, bulimia, and binge eating disorder (B.E.D.) and some more rare disorders. Some people dip into these illnesses for varying periods (months or years) and then recover, some swap between different eating disorders, other illnesses, some remain ill for many years, some recover, and some die.

In the Western world, *using strict diagnostic criteria*, the prevalence (actual number of current sufferers) of eating disorders runs at 0.28% for anorexia and 1% for bulimia.[2] Between 5% and 15% of sufferers are male.[3] These figures may well represent an open minority of those suffering, and there are statistics that claim much higher rates. It is also probable that the true figures of those with eating disorders could be higher, due to the denial that anything is wrong, fear of humiliation, or other reasons for inhibition about coming forward with

---

[1] http://www.b-eat.co.uk/Home
[2] Hoek, HW (1995). *The distribution of eating disorders.* Brownell KD, & Fairburn CG, (Eds.) *Eating Disorders and Obesity: A comprehensive handbook.* New York: Guilford Press, p.207-211.
[3] Andersen AE. (1995) *Eating disorders in males.* In: Brownell KD, Fairburn CG, (Eds). *Eating Disorders and Obesity: a comprehensive handbook.* New York: Guilford Press, p.177-87.

their illness, particularly those ashamed of making themselves vomit or use laxatives, and men who are ashamed to have a "woman's illness."

On top of these figures are people with disordered eating who do not fit the strict criteria, but who still suffer deeply: including those with eating disorder not otherwise specified[4] (E.D.N.O.S.) and of course binge eating disorder (B.E.D.) What is more, although (large, long-term) prospective cohort studies for eating disorders are unfeasible, retrospective analysis shows that the incidence (the number of *new* cases) of these "modern" illnesses is continuously increasing all around the world.[5]

As stated, eating disorders have the equally highest mortality rate of all psychiatric illnesses (equal with bipolar disorder, standing at up to 20% of sufferers). It is essentially noteworthy that depression (sometimes manic depression/bipolar disorder) seems to occur *ubiquitously* in people with eating disorders – thus the risk of death due to depression (suicide) is compounded by the physical risk of death due to the eating disorder. The effects of starving, purging, other psychiatric disorders and therefore suicide: can be lethal. Five to ten percent of anorectics die within ten years of onset, 18-20% die within twenty years of onset, but it is vital to note that *with* treatment this is reduced to 2-3%. (ANAD[6]). Over a third of victims end up living with illness long-term despite treatment, a third recover somewhat but still struggle, and a third make a full

---

[4] EDNOS describes people with disordered eating who do not fit strict criteria for another Eating Disorder. This is discussed in more detail later.
[5] Same as ref. no. 48: Hoek, HW (1995), p.208-209.
[6] ANAD - National Association of Anorexia nervosa and Associated Disorders.

recovery. These percentages can be waved around without thinking about the huge number of real live, fantastic human beings, together with their families and friends, who all suffer, and some die. I lost a friend, Claire, a keen runner. She was 31 when she dropped down dead, no warnings.

In your lifetime, eating disorder charities estimate that at least 50,000 people will die as a direct result of anorexia or bulimia. By this I mean deaths due to *acute* illness, including but not exclusively: literal starvation, organ failure (e.g. renal failure), gastrointestinal crisis (e.g. gastric dilatation leading to a ruptured stomach), heart attacks (arrhythmias are common, particularly conduction defects and ventricular arrhythmias), electrolyte imbalance (usually when purging is present causing low potassium), dehydration, and not uncommonly suicide.

This does not take into account *many* lives that are shortened by damage done to the body of someone who lives with one of these illnesses long term, or who dies after recovery or partial-recovery, but still much younger than they otherwise would die. Nor does it include morbidity and mortality due to obesity linked to B.E.D. or other eating disorders. Many thousands die from complications of obesity as a result of binge eating disorder. For all eating disorders, *quality* of life is *very* much reduced: although this can be invisible to the sufferer, seen as a worthwhile trade off, or beyond control. For other sufferers, their entrapment within a reduced quality life is all too apparent. This reduced quality of life includes psychological factors such as depression, with physical problems such as osteoporosis (the thinning of bones usually found in old age) and infertility. Any treatment or harm minimisation strategies must include psychological and physical risk management – and be undertaken with great patience by all involved.

Despite the high morbidity and mortality associated with eating disorders, I believe that they are effective coping mechanisms: enabling *unbelievable* pain and torment to be endured. Much like someone using heroin, alcohol or self-harm, these people are using food control as their last resort: due to predisposing and precipitating factors that mean they "choose" this particular form of escape. This happens without any comprehension of the price that must be paid, until it is far too late. It was how I was so enticed: I believe my anorexia saved my life (in the early years). It numbed my mania, depression and the rigorous bullying I was subjected to. Unfortunately, once embraced, eating disorders *trap* you and add to your distress, as surely as you don't feed your body, they take control and feed off you like a parasite. Only those people so entrapped (past or present) will really *know* what that feels like to exist in that state. It kept me trapped until I left Oxford, age 28.

Eating disorders are not merely "slimming disorders," they are far more complex than such a superficial name suggests. Vanity and stupidity are *not* causal factors; extreme self-hatred is. People with eating disorders tend to be intelligent and sensitive, perhaps overly so. Many are perfectionists and set themselves very high (unattainable) standards: thus feel disappointed in themselves. The term "clinical perfectionism" has been coined to describe people whose perfectionism is so absolute and inflexible that it causes them problems, such as mental health problems. All eating disorders

Reflective Reflections

have [7]*predisposing, precipitating* and *maintaining* factors, which vary person to person: although many of common factors are the found in most sufferers. Onset, for example, tends to be during adolescence. A period of dieting prior to onset is almost ubiquitous, as is the presence of a mood disorder. These and many other aspects form a complicated and unique mixture in each sufferer: resulting in a great sense of hopelessness, which needs great skill to treat, and powerful strength to survive. Fortunately people who develop eating disorders tend to be bright, resilient, insightful (eventually), and very strong willed – were they not so strong willed they would never have managed to develop an eating disorder in the first place. This means they will only recover when they truly want to, and even then it can take years, needing assistance, patience and effort.

Predisposing factors include a mixture of *nature:* genetics, a family history of psychiatric illness, neurochemistry and physiology (e.g. a predisposition to obesity)[8] and *nurture* (the family environment, social factors and stresses, and traumatic life events: such as abuse, rape, feeling controlled, psychiatric illness, bullying and psychological issues etc.) Traumatic life events may be well intentioned and thought to be harmless: such as a parent stressing the importance of maintaining a healthy weight, the message of being healthy being twisted into one of being only valid when losing weight. Families tend to eat in the same way, so

---

[7] Explained thus in group therapy to myself and other patients at the Oxford Adult Eating Disorders Service, Cotswold House, Warneford Hospital, Oxford.

[8] Cooper Z., *The Development and maintenance of Eating Disorders*. In: Brownell KD, Fairburn CG, (Eds). Eating Disorders and Obesity: a comprehensive handbook. New York: Guilford Press, p.199-205.

a neurotic mother who diets may unintentionally pass this behaviour on to her children.

Identical twins are more likely to develop the same eating disorder than non-identical twins – even if separated at birth. However, not all identical twins suffer the same (or any) eating disorder. Thus twin studies prove that genetics play a role but do not solely explain why some people develop anorexia or bulimia. Eating disorders also run in families; but not all relations suffer: this suggests a complex polygenic (many genes are involved in the process) link that must be combined with other lifetime factors before an eating disorder is precipitated in those who are already predisposed.

The line between predisposing and precipitating factors can get blurry. As with predisposing factors, precipitating factors can include physical events such as a period of mental or physical illness, especially experiencing depression, manic depression, sexual abuse, physical abuse, emotional abuse, bullying, neglect, bereavement, issues of control, issues of leaving home, and growing up: either in the form of one incident, or the build up of continued trauma …the list literally is endless. Generally precipitating factors are the proverbial "final straw," the event(s) that suddenly or eventually causes someone (consciously and/or unconsciously) to think, "f*ck it" and throw themselves off the precipice.

However, a crucial point to note is that for many sufferers, there is no reason (or reasons) that they can place as the cause(s) of their illness. That doesn't mean there are no reasons, it just means that the victim may be unaware of them at present, and/or feel that her/his problems are unimportant, and do not warrant them "failing" by becoming ill. Apart from the more "typical" causes, there are so many roots towards this dissonance; it is impossible to cover them all, but all are *equally valid*. This is one reason why psychotherapy is such a helpful treatment in eating disorders: self-awareness is of paramount importance to recovery, as is self-kindness.

Maintaining factors include all physical and psychological issues that make breaking free from the eating disorder difficult once it becomes established. These include a continued low self-esteem, ever-increasing dichotomous thinking (black or white, yes or no, everything is in extremes with fewer and fewer grey areas). This dichotomous thinking "helps" the anorectic because it makes decisions easy – there is no wondering whether to eat for example a chocolate bar, there is no "shall I" or "shan't I" debate, there is a simple "no" and doesn't even have to be worried about – This can be applied to all areas of life, not just food, making decision making rigid, controlled, but feeling safe for the anorectic. I am 35, no longer anorectic by any means, but I don't go out to eat because I get embarrassed to be seen eating, I don't even eat with my family – factors linger still.

Back to maintaining factors, there is also always a large helping of guilt, non-resolution of issues that actually caused the illness, and new factors such as the act of eating becoming mentally and physically more difficult – actually painful, an addiction to starving – some people report feeling high, I used to love feeling hungry, losing weight and seeing the numbers go down. Purging can be addictive because some people associate it with getting rid of their crappy feelings at the same time, and of course if you purge you have to vomit or take some measure that fills in time – which can feel like a blessing when time drags. Starvation syndrome (obsessive thoughts about food, cravings) …again, the list is extensive is very powerful at numbing the mind of the eating disordered person from things they don't want to think about.

Unfortunately eating disorders are also maintained by apparently positive factors: enjoying being thin, people commenting positively on weight loss (at first), wearing small clothes, getting positive feedback from some people, maybe even being forced to be thin for work (if you are a ballerina, model or actress – or any job where you feel your small size is beneficial), or even making a silent statement that you are disappearing, enjoying *feeling* in control, and if a person purges, the enjoyment surrounding being able to eat anything in a binge… all of which are actually harmful and dangerous.

The interesting question becomes, why food? Why an eating disorder? Why not drink, do drugs, indulge in lots of (risky) sex? The media and society are partly to blame, although I personally do not believe the media *cause* eating disorders in the absence of other serious problems and risk factors. The idea that "Fat is bad and thin is good" or "You can never be *too* thin" is still pervasive in today's society and is decidedly unhelpful. Are our clothes made to fit us or are we supposed to change ourselves to fit in a certain size? The dreaded size zero. (Size 4 in UK sizing). It has been the same all my life, and I had made it my personal crusade to fit in; then I became too tired to dance that dance, no more than a puppeteer being controlled by some dark master. Cutting the strings by which I dangled felt like snipping off an arm or a leg each time. I lost years of my life to eating disorders… Years I will never regain, and did harm to myself that I can never undo.

Reflective Reflections

Some people are without doubt discriminated against because of their weight. Indeed complete strangers can hurl abuse based purely on size, without provocation. This can be overt, bitchy, weak, violent, or just a subversive giggle with a pointed finger: I guarantee that the victim feels abominable – even if their head is held high, and a dignified lack-of-hearing acquired temporarily. Thin is associated with being successful, beautiful and desirable. This idea can be clung to by a lonely, depressed/bipolar/anxious and other impressionable people who want to be perfect and fit in.

Dieting is the leading cause of eating disorders: although of course, you can't develop anorexia, (i.e. become an anorectic[9]) unless you diet, and you are unlikely to obsess about food and/or end up bingeing and vomiting unless driven by hunger - at least initially. Most people who develop an eating disorder do so after an initial attempt to diet normally.[10] It is my opinion that many people assume dieting to be a simple matter of eating less, and *that the psychological impact of eating less (at various weights) is given poor if any consideration.* True: some people desire anorexia – I did; and some think bulimia is their own fantastic, secret discovery – I did. I had no idea what I was letting myself in for. Any euphoria is short lived.

---

[9] By definition, "an Anorectic" is *a person who suffers from Anorexia*. Colloquially the word Anorexic is used for most descriptions, but being pedantic and cautious, I prefer to define people as <u>someone</u> *with an illness*, not just as an illness. Both are understood; the term Anorexic is used more commonly.

[10] Polivy, J. Herman, CP. (1995). *Dieting and its relation to Eating Disorders*. Brownell KD, & Fairburn CG, (Eds.) *Eating Disorders and Obesity: A comprehensive handbook.* New York: Guilford Press, p.84

Many people are insecure and losing weight seems to be the panacea to end all problems, which of course it does not. Millions of people diet without getting an eating disorder, so not all dieting leads to eating disorders, but millions of people are unhappy with their weight and blame their size for problems in their life. Take some facts from American research.[11] The average woman is 5"4' and weighs 140 pounds. The average model is 5"11' and weighs 117 pounds. Fashion models are thinner than 98% of American women; and the 2 percent who are thinner than the models probably include eating disorder sufferers. Look at the (mainly female) non-existent Hollywood stars on the big screen. An unfortunately large number: 80% of American women are dissatisfied with their appearance.

So what about their Body Mass Index – BMI[12]? Are these weights healthy? A simple calculation reveals that (by any diagnostic criteria used), these models have *anorexic* BMIs (under 17.5, the cut off point for anorexia) of just 16.3; compared to the average BMI of 24, which is a "normal" healthy weight – but still leaving $^4/_5$ths of these women dissatisfied with their figure. In the Western world, at least 50% of women admit to being on a diet at any given time.[13] Since diets almost

---

[11] Smolak, L. (1996). National Eating Disorders Association/Next Door Neighbours puppet guide book.

[12] **BMI** means **Body Mass Index**, and is a measurement of weight that takes into consideration the height of a person – since tall people should weigh more. Your BMI is calculated by **dividing your weight in kg**, by your **height in metres^2** For example a woman weighing 65kg who is 1.65m tall has a BMI of $65/(1.65)^2 = 23.9$. For women, a normal BMI is between 19-24, for men it's 20-25. For people recovering from and Eating disorder, a BMI of 20 is usually aimed for. A BMI > 30 is classed as "clinically obese."

[13] Brownell KD (1995) *Effects of Weight Cycling on Metabolism, Heath, and Psychological issues.* In: Brownell KD, Fairburn CG,

universally make people miserable, and some people obsessive: the fact that dieting is so widespread is a sad fact.

What scares me the most is how young the non-issue of weight is being embraced by our children? Beliefs developed so young are hard to challenge or change – however much damage they may be doing. Research[14] shows that 80% of children have been on a diet by the time that they have reached the fourth grade (age 9-10). Over half of 9-10 year old girls feel better about themselves if they are on a miserable diet.

I was once that 9 year old. I remember hoping that in the future, no child would have to go through what I did; surely society would recognise such a mistake? But now it seems that more children are weight conscious than ever: a *tragedy*. I strongly believe that more education (at childhood level) is needed to warn people about the dangers of diets – and that this should be done by encouraging people to eat more healthy foods and exercise for fun, rather than labelling foods as "bad."

As mentioned briefly: going on a diet doesn't *just* affect your physical body (metabolism and health, e.g. bones, possibly for the worse): it affects your *mind* and *personality*. This is an area desperate for more research. To put it bluntly: dieting makes you miserable. If you fail to lose weight, you feel bad. If you do succeed in losing weight, feelings of bitter despair follow if weight is regained, and at least 95% of dieters regain all their

---

(Eds). *Eating Disorders and Obesity: a comprehensive handbook.* New York: Guilford Press, 1995, p.56-59

[14] Mellin L McNutt S Hu Y Schreiber GB Crawford P & Obarzanek E (1991). *A longitudinal study of the dietary practices of black and white girls 9 and 10 years old at enrollment: The NHLBI growth and health study.* Journal of Adolescent Health, p. 27-37.

lost weight, plus a bit extra. Dieting is more likely to lead to gaining weight than losing it, and more likely to make people unhappy.[15]

The act of dieting causes people to think and dream more about food and eating. This is a physiological and psychological reaction to starvation that has been seen in starvation studies[16]. The less someone eats the more they find themselves thinking about food, eating slowly, allowed food being treated as far more precious, eventually obsessing about it. In someone with an eating disorder this preoccupation with food can be extreme: I would spend an hour eating one fat-free yoghurt with the wrong end of a teaspoon to make sure I only took tiny mouthfuls. Also I recall nightmares of dreams being chased around by food, or having just eaten (binged on) a load of food, with nothing I could do about it. The conscious day was even more painful. I still get those dreams now, even though I am recovered.

Some opinions voiced about eating disorders are outdated and seem to come from an overly condescending, patriarchal medical profession. Telling someone who has been sexually abused that she doesn't want to grow up and leave the protective home environment, or have relationships can devastate her/him. (Granted, the professional may well know nothing of the abuse). I craved independence and respect, but was made to feel as though some men had just decided it was a silly disease of vanity, cured by factory-style re-feeding and weight gain, by force if

---

[15] Wilson, GT. (1995). *The controversy over dieting.* Brownell KD, & Fairburn CG, (Eds.) *Eating Disorders and Obesity: a comprehensive handbook.* New York: Guilford Press, p.87-91

[16] The classic example being the Keys et al., (1950) *Minnesota Human Starvation Study.*

necessary: actually the *worst* thing you can do to an anorectic.

There is some truth in *some* cases, is that anorexia results from a girl trying to avoid growing up, stopping her periods, and not developing secondary sexual characteristics. I do not doubt that esteemed (male) researchers came upon this theory when they treated patients who gave reasons to give this explanation. I do agree that *some* young women find it difficult when they develop sexual characteristics, but it is a rather large stretch to suggest this means they do not want to grow up and have sex. Some of us are desperate to grow up and be independent (and have sex).

I have asked a large number of people, anorectics and bulimics of all weights, including many of low-weights, but not a single one consciously wished to remain child-like, although some physically appeared that way. In many cases, including mine, the exact opposite is the case. I never wanted to return to my childhood, in fact I couldn't wait to grow up and be independent. Somehow, despite this, independence eludes me and others like me.

But I agree that whilst some sufferers do not want to be sexual beings – some do, some are more likely to involve themselves in sex if they feel thin, and some are less likely – for fear of being discovered as ill, and some do not connect sex/relationships with their weight to a great extent. However, the same is true of those who are normal weight and those who are overweight – in other words: being intimate can be difficult irrespective of weight.

It is distressing when "outsiders" say *to the family* of the eating disorder victim things like, "Why didn't you see it?" "I wouldn't have let it get to this stage," or worst of all "It's your fault you should make her eat or stop her throwing up." Some of this might be said behind the victim's parents' backs. I would respond: how can you possibly understand the dynamics going on in someone else's family where an evil illness is at play? The person with an eating disorder is a bright person, going to great lengths to hide their illness, and even when it becomes more and more obvious, they will have an answer for everything – and will be forced by their disease into manipulating their family. Don't *ever* judge other families like this; it compounds the problems. They have enough to deal with. Even if they were on top of their child's illness quickly, they may not be able to control its pathway. Friends and family are always desperate to help; yet are powerless to suddenly make everything OK. Eating disorders are bastard diseases.

Trust me when I say that the family of a person with an eating disorder do *everything* in their power to help. Some things are beyond help; some things take time. Families try persuasion, they try anger, they block access to the bathroom, and they cook food they think will please their loved one: the temptation possibly triggering a bulimic's binge and/or angering an anorexic trying to maintain "control." Families seek the help of medical professionals, even hospital, but little can be done without the cooperation of the victim – especially once they turn 18. The battles that take place within the homes of families with eating disorders are as vicious and manipulative as they come – it is a battle for *power*, and it is one that the eating disorder often wins, at least for a period of time. The sufferer and the family lose.

Some parents *are* irresponsible to a degree, especially with young sufferers. Many family members try to be helpful, but instead do damage. My parents describe feeling baffled and like they were "walking on eggshells" around me, waiting for me to explode or hurt myself. Parents must continue, for as long as need be, to support (emotionally, and financially if need be) their child if he or she is to have a chance of recovery. Recovery does not happen until the person is ready for it, and nothing you do, or don't do, can work miracles. Never give up on your child.

෴

A major difference between an anorectic and a bulimic is that an anorectic's control and fears mainly surround *weight*, whereas a bulimic's control, lack-of-control, and fears surround *food*. However: *food and weight are both issues to both groups.*

෴

One of the worst things about eating disorders is the frustration for family, friends and professionals surrounding the sufferer being unable to convince her/him that she is ill, that there is a problem, that the perceived control is actually them being manipulated by the illness. Confrontation is ugly, the eating disorder turning the sufferer into a vicious, angry, fearful person. People who care tend to shy away for fear of making things worse, or because they feel powerless to help. Eating disorders are very cunning at achieving isolation of the sufferer: the illness becomes the closest "friend," the victim *absolutely* convinced she/he is in control. Many regret their angry behaviour. Many regret their illness-induced arrogance. I know I do. I used to think other people were stupid for eating. Of course, this means the eating disorder wins: until the person suffering is so poorly that they recognise they are ill and are ready and able to accept help.

The worst thing about eating disorders is the fact that even after a sufferer accepts there is a problem and understands that their control is an illusion: once they try to change, once they seek help, once they desire recovery; change may be painfully slow, non-existent or too late. Eating disorders are a fierce battle for *control* between victim, the illness, and all the people caught in the fallout. The illness does not like to lose its powerful grip but recovery is possible.

The best way to treat an eating disorder is to never develop one.

Chapter 1: Anorexia nervosa.

> "What really raises one's indignation against suffering is not suffering intrinsically, but the senselessness of suffering."
>
> ❧ Friedrich Nietzsche (1844-1900.).

People who develop anorexia (anorectics) crave validation and understanding, but get little of each. They also desire control within their life, but instead are controlled – overly so, even with the best of intentions by the controller or situation. They are intelligent and want to help people, but their own health does not matter. *Anorexia* (which means loss of appetite) is actually a misnomer because actually the illness is a daily battle with their appetite and self-induced starvation syndrome, although admitting to feeling hunger may not be possible, or even recognised by the victim as time passes. Indeed, knowing or admitting to any feelings can be extremely difficult; depression is common, suicide possible. Death from literal starvation or purgative behaviour is common.

Remember - the mortality rate for untreated anorexia is equally the highest as for any other psychiatric disorder (20%) and 2% of those treated still die.

Anorectics are typically stronger willed than most people (which can be a bad thing as well as good), and anorectics are definitely able to deal better with the effects of starvation. Indeed some anorectics claim to be addicted to starvation, and the "high" it can sometimes produce. I never felt it, despite long periods of partial and total starvation. However I did like feeling hungry as it made me feel mentally powerful and also physically weak, which I liked because I felt I deserved punishment. It is also very effective at diverting attention onto food and eating instead of feeling real (unpleasant) emotions. Epidemiological studies show that the prevalence of people with anorexia nervosa over the last 20 years has increased - The reason behind this is not known, but cultural influences are suggested as all or part of the cause.[17] It is also likely that the illness is now much more easily recognised, hence recorded.

The **DSM-IV Criteria for Anorexia nervosa**[18] are the world-standardised criteria used for diagnosis of mental disorders, although you may also find the **ICD-10** useful. (For a comparison of both DSM-VI and ICD-10[19]).

❖ **List of Diagnostic Symptoms of Anorexia nervosa**

> ❖ Inability to maintain body weight at a minimally normal weight for age and height (e.g. weight loss less than 85% of

---

[17] Wilfley D.E. Rodin J., (1995). *Cultural Influences on Eating Diorders*. In K.D. Brownell & C.G. Fairburn (Eds.) *Eating Disorders and Obesity: A comprehensive handbook* (p. 78). New York: Guilford.

[18] Absolutely strict diagnostic criteria that are used by physicians worldwide are found in the DSM-IV *Diagnostic and Statistical Manual of Mental Disorders, Fourth Edition*, (1994). Copyright American Psychiatric Association. For Anorexia nervosa see p. 544-545.

[19] Garfinkel P.E., (1995), *Classification and Diagnosis of Eating Disorders*. In: Brownell KD, Fairburn CG, (Eds). *Eating Disorders and Obesity: a comprehensive handbook*. New York: Guilford Press, 1995, p.125-134.

that expected or failure to make expected weight gain during period of growth, leading to body weight less than 85% of that expected. More recently a BMI of 17.5 or less is being used*).

❖ Marked trepidation about gaining weight or becoming fat, even though actually underweight, and under eating or over exercising.

❖ Disturbance about the way one's body weight or shape is perceived with excessive influence of body weight or shape on self-evaluation, or outright denial of the seriousness of the current low body weight.

❖ In postmenarchal females, amenorrhea i.e. the absence of at least three consecutive cycles. (And the woman must not be on the pill, which can cause bleeding despite anorexia).

*Note that the weight/height ratio of a BMI less than or equal to 17.5 is now often used as the "benchmark" weight for a strict diagnosis of anorexia. Using the BMI takes into account the patient's height. Obviously weight cannot be ignored, especially in emaciated patients, but I would maintain that weight is mostly irrelevant: *certainly extraneous with respect to measuring suffering*. The more the medical/psychological professions place importance on weight, the more eating disorder sufferers do the same – and it is a misappropriation of time and energy by all.

Do not look at the above list and assume you are not ill. A friend of mine is 47 and has had anorexia since she was 10. She denies her seriously anorexic status on the basis that she continues to menstruate – just one example of how it is important to *not* self-diagnose. See an expert.

Anorexia is then further specified into purging or non-purging type.

> ❖ *Non-purging type. (Restricting type).* Younger anorectics often begin their illness "career" with this form of anorexia, where the only means of control used are not-eating and maybe some non-purging (e.g. exercise, some drugs like speed) forms of controlling weight.
>
> ❖ *Purging[20] type (unrestricting type, binge eating type, anorectic bulimia).* There are many ways to *seemingly* purge a body of energy, such as vomiting, laxatives and diuretics. An anorectic who uses them might do so following unwanted, (possibly forced) "normal" food intake and/or bingeing, and will have a diagnosis of anorexia nervosa, purging type. (Note that "normal" eating may be perceived as a binge to an anorectic, the term binge is

---

[20] In Eating Disorders, "purging," means the act of washing out, giving a sense of "cleansing" unwanted elements from the body, usually ingested food. There are many methods by which this is done.

somewhat subjective). Enemas may also be self administered to supposedly aid weight loss.

It is slightly unclear where exercise fits – i.e. is it healthy? It is always individual, but exercise can become very problematic, and in many cases is a punitive and/or addictive form of weight control. Personally I reached the stage where I was getting up at 3am to give me time to cycle 50 miles before work when I lived in Oxford. Purging methods will be covered in more detail in the bulimia section. Note that whilst various drugs, especially appetite suppressants might be used, and whilst these cannot be considered purgative: they can be an important part of the pathology. (Some drugs *are* purgative; depending on mechanism of action).

o **Predisposing, precipitating and maintaining factors.**

Predisposing factors in general have already been discussed in some detail, and all still apply here. But the question begs, why does one person turn to anorexia, whereas another becomes bulimic or ill in some other way. Again, partly this will be down to genetics (predisposition). Further predisposing and ultimately precipitating factors might include any way in which a strange relationship is developed around food. This might come from watching your anorectic mum pick at her food, or being bullied for your weight causing you to hate yourself or being watched whilst eating. Or you may love eating, get comfort from it, and hate yourself for doing so... The list is endless.

Anorectics are usually high achieving, idealistic, perhaps naïve, and perfectionists: indeed many are "clinical perfectionists[21]." A friend told me (some years after recovery) that he had been afraid of being labelled as gay. I bit my tongue whilst thinking about my great gay friends, but had to accept that he felt unable to cope with taunts he might receive: and it is a valid point. All people with eating disorders come with an overly large helping of low self-esteem, even self-hatred, and a high incidence of other mental health problems, mainly mood disorders and alcoholism.

Maintaining[22] factors in anorexia can become very serious and include both psychological and physical. As mentioned, particularly in anorexia as opposed to other eating disorders, the sufferer may not be willing/able to accept they are ill. The longer the illness continues, the more severe the weight loss, physical damage, and ability of the sufferer to change their behaviour and beliefs. Many play all kinds of games to avoid weight gain. Psychotherapy is difficult, especially in a low weight patient who sees life from a "simple" dichotomous viewpoint, whereby they are right, the world is wrong.

Dichotomous thinking: as explained, so-called "black-or-white" or "all-or-nothing" thinking is common in all people with eating disorders. It may seem "easy" to see the world as good or bad: the thinking and definitions more simple as there are fewer options to consider. Thin is good vs. fat is bad. Not eating is good vs. eating is bad. Everyone else is wonderful vs. I am terrible and

---

[21] Perfectionism becomes an obsessive feature that has a detrimental effect on wellbeing.

[22] Me, it happened to me. Also see Marilyn Duker and Roger Slade, *Anorexia and Bulimia nervosa: How to help.*

unworthy. There is no question as to whether to eat one or three apples, no choice as to accept the offer of a crisp, drink or sweet from a friend. The answer is a resounding "No" to all bad foods, and a hesitant yes to as few good foods as possible. (For example I spent years on fruit, soya milk and tuna). Eating "bad" foods is simply not an option.

Generally, the lower the weight of an anorectic, the more all-or-nothing their thinking is likely to be. Gaining weight is bad, bad, bad; and actions must be taken to avoid it – consciously and even unconsciously. Negotiating a change from anorectic behaviour that feels safe is very difficult, especially if the victim can only see their problems in such a way that leaves them only two options: remain a good anorectic, or become bad and massively obese. There are no grades of fatness, normal weight is still fat, only underweight is "good," and the more underweight, the "safer" it feels.

Physically, because the anorectic's stomach has shrunk, and gastric emptying is slowed, eating food is actually physically uncomfortable. This is reversible when proper eating is restored. (Metoclopramide can be prescribed short-term to help treat this, although it tends to be left to nature: the human digestive system is very capable of restoring itself).

It is also true that once a person gets used to being thin, gaining weight feels like a failure. If clothes feel tighter, it's a failure, if control is relaxed, it's a failure, and if weight goes up, it's a failure – even when desperate to recover, these feelings remain. Buying newer clothes is emotionally painful. It can feel as though being "empty" is the only way to be comfortable; eating anything can result in feeling, actually (although a delusion) *seeing* your body grow or *feeling* heavy. As the day progresses, anything eaten is added up – by whatever score system the person uses: calories, feelings, tape measures, tightness of clothes, appearance in a mirror – hence eating tends to be delayed as late as possible. Obsessing over bodily functions is common, as is a life that is chaotic in many areas, causing work problems, relationship problems, etc.

Even when a sufferer wants to recover, they find living with illness and/or fighting for recovery extremely stressful. Improvement feels like it is taking forever, or it's impossible: but people can and do recover and/or progress.

o **Delving a little deeper into the behaviours in anorexia nervosa: warning signs.**

There are a number of strange behaviours: some or all that are found in anorectics (*and* people with other eating disorders – there is a lot of overlap). These almost universally worsen/maintain the deleterious progression of the illness - which you the sufferer, or friends, family, teachers and careers can spot. The earlier you spot and challenge a person's behaviour (or your own), the greater the chance of a recovery. Don't be afraid to be hated, or to create a scene: you may hear some very hateful comments back – these are not your loved one, these are the anorexia speaking. Don't avoid taking responsibility for yourself if you are ill. The anorexia is very manipulative of the sufferer, and making the victim a master manipulator of others such as family who are scared.

It may seem easier to think that you, or someone you love, are healthy, than face the harsh fact that a serious, life-threatening *mental* disorder is present and needs addressing. I fooled people for years; it was easy – or if they were not fooled they said nothing, which still mean the anorexia won the battle that day. Worst of all, I fooled myself, or rather, allowed my anorexia to trick me. It may have been a "useful" survival strategy, I am certain there were better options! Don't take the easier path; don't be/pretend to be fooled: *see beyond expecting only a skeleton or death, and see these other signs also.* Don't be deceived: the longer the illness goes on, the harder it is to treat. Try to only become angry at the anorexia, not yourself, and/or not the person *who is ill.*

Anorectics are hungry, subject to starvation syndrome, and will fill up on diet coke, coffee, water, over the counter appetite suppressants, and maybe even prescription or street drugs that curb/eliminate appetite. This behaviour may also be found in bulimia victims when not bingeing. When extremely ill, even fluid intake may be measured and restricted: dehydration is one possible cause of death in eating disorder sufferers.

Starvation syndrome causes preoccupation with food which might explain why a typical anorectic (or bulimic) will hoard food, read about food, shop for food, cook food - usually for others, and constantly think about food, in fact, will do everything with food except eat it properly. Such thinking pushes out some or all other negative thoughts: which is why anorexia works as a survival strategy for other problems. It is not uncommon for family members of an anorectic to gain a little weight because they are so being well fed. This can carry on into later life, with an anorectic mother overfeeding (or worse underfeeding) her children. In my family, my anorectic Grandma would over feed her whole family including her grandchildren. She must have spent many hours preparing for every Sunday's ritualistic gathering; the food on offer was quite overwhelming.

When you are starving, watching others eat food is mesmerizing. This includes food you have prepared, or just food in general, even on TV or in public. It is almost like a type of surrogate-eating in order to satisfy the eating disorder victim's appetite and hunger. (Appetite and hunger are not the same thing). If someone within sight is eating, I guarantee an anorectic will always notice, watch, and think about it. I still watch people eat and pretend to eat: it's compulsive. We also notice when people on TV shows pretend to eat – picking at food – it's almost a game.

Obviously, over time, there will be some weight change. But this weight change can be or appear minimal, especially if it is hidden well by the sufferer by wearing larger clothes, or several layers of clothes. Nor should weight be the only or indeed main indicator of severity of illness. All non-purging and most purging anorectics lose weight, but the rate at which this can happen varies tremendously, and weight may increase and decrease many times. When living with a person it can be easy to miss small daily changes. Losing weight quickly is a poor indicator of a good prognosis – but not an indomitable reason for giving up. I knew a girl who lost a vast amount of weight in a tiny period of time but recovered quickly – her mind unpolluted by kcals and fat content of food, so new to the 'game' was she.

Outward signs of illness usually become obviously visible. Thinness that is flaunted or
hidden; lanugo hair (a soft downy hair) may be seen on the back, arms, stomach and even face of victims. This is an adaptation to cold; all anorectics feel the cold badly because they lack fat under their skin to keep

them warm and they are starving. Skin pallor changes: people look pale, tired, the way skin wrinkles around the mouth is typical and the dark yet wide (staring) eyes are a dead giveaway to an experienced observer. Anorectics find it hard to sit still, partly because their bony bodies feel uncomfortable, partly anxiety, and partly excess adrenaline (epinephrine). This adrenaline fuels the starving body, and causes or worsens anxiety and insomnia.

Obviously with anorexia nervosa, it does eventually become overtly apparent that the person is ill; however all sorts of excuses may be made, such as a bout of illness, or insistence that there is some physical/metabolic problem. If need be, anorectics will defend their right to starve (to their death) and will be defensive about many facets of their life. Routines will be important, sometimes to great extremes: such as keeping a daily record of what time they wake up, how long they sleep, even when they switch a light on, anything eaten, anything drunk, exercise, purging methods (if applicable), circumference of waist/arms/legs, and of course their weight, possibly measured several times a day, and other body checking/evaluations... so that any increase or decrease in weight can be understood and counteracted. This obsession takes up a great deal of time, all day if you need it to, it seems to make sense at the time and is a way of avoiding even thinking about other problems.

All of which brings me onto drugs. Be it purgative or to dampen down appetite for abstainers, there are a number of drugs used by people with eating disorders to lose weight. Speed and cocaine are common street drugs used, particularly amongst certain professions. Legal appetite suppressants can be bought in chemists

– they are fairly useless. Chewing gum (sugar free, but containing sorbitol a laxative) is also used to take the edge off hunger. There are horror stories of people eating non-food items such as tissues because they were hungry and didn't want to eat anything calorific, i.e. "bad."

Do anorectics eat? People think they don't, but they do – in fact what an anorectic *does* eat might well be the focus for their *whole day*. All the food they do actually eat becomes very important to them, and must be "perfect." Eating food may become ritualised, such as cutting the food into small pieces, adding lots of salt or strong substances like English mustard (which burns), not touching food to the lips, and setting a time period after which food will be thrown away. An anorectic (maybe *you*) who thinks she or he is eating properly may be vastly underestimating what is normal.

All anorectics become subject to starvation syndrome (as discussed) causing them to focus their thoughts on food and weight obsessively. I remember daily freezing fat-free yoghurt until it was solid, and then eating it by scraping it slowly with the wrong-end of a teaspoon – a ritual taking an hour or more. I always left it as late as I could in the day, and spent the whole day looking forward to my evening mini-meal, feeling guilty at the same time.

I used to become a nightmare daughter – in order to make my tuna and tomato salad, or my tuna and tomato sandwich (no spread, diet bread that I didn't eat, lots of smelly onion), I banished everyone from the kitchen so that they couldn't watch me, then I had to scrub the surfaces clean, the plate clean, the fork clean, with a clean dishcloth and lots of soap – I was scared of contamination from cheese, or butter, or oil... Later when I became purging type, I left food all over the house in a terrific mess. One anxiety was gone, but only because I replaced it with a far worse one. And when not bingeing, I still had to scrub all surfaces before I touched them, I wouldn't open the fridge, in fact I wouldn't even go in the kitchen in case I inhaled food molecules. (How can that not be classed as delusional?) If I smelled cooking when walking through town, I would cross over the road. I wonder when does anxiety about food become delusional in the psychiatric sense of the word?

People mistakenly think that if they see someone appear to eat normally at one time, or a few times, then they are "fine." But the truth may be that that food is vomited, secreted into pockets/the dog/the floor/anywhere but the stomach, exercised away, or the only thing that is eaten that day/week. As a teenager, I used to get up early so that I could go down to the kitchen and bang a few cupboards, then mash up some cereal in bowl, getting some right up to the rim, and then "casually" leave it for someone else to see and so think I had eaten.

Some anorectics eat their daily energy in the form of eating very small amounts of high fat foods, but this is rare. Some eat small amounts of normal food. Most eat small/normal/abnormal amounts of low-fat, low-calorie, low-carbohydrate food, (often varying with the most recent in vogue diet-craze) such as carrots, lettuce etc. Rarely, some anorectics turn orange from the beta-carotene in all the carrots they eat.

Mood changes are common – not restricted to depression and anxiety, which may or may not be hidden well, but other mood swings also. The anorectic may seem happy (especially early on in the illness, and when losing weight). It is not uncommon for battles over food to go on within the family. Anger on both sides is common when faced with eating when food it is offered, or it is a family event, or the alarmed parent is demanding their child eat. Put bluntly, an anorectic can become unswerving, uncooperative, and manipulative to those around them – I did. (And calling myself a bitch at those times is probably too polite).

Some sufferers are more subtly manipulative: I was less so. It is hard not to be angry with someone manipulating you. I hated behaving badly but anything was preferable to eating food. I say all this not to condemn the anorectic, rather to explain such extreme mood swings that are part of the illness, not personal flaws of the victim. In such cases it may be helpful to personify the anorexia, and *be angry with the anorexia, not the ill person*.

A person's career may be a risk factor: I know a number of ballerinas who seem to be totally scarred by their career choice; an anorectic weight is openly demanded. And then there are models and people in the media spotlight…

Claire, an anorectic runner I knew died from her illness at the age of 31: her belief was that the thinner she was, the faster she could run. A person running competitively may lose weight or be very slim even if eating – seems reasonable doesn't it? Indeed it is usual for competitive runners to be very lean. In an eating disorder victim, this allows an unhealthy exercise addiction to be explained away concurrently.

By no means do I mean all people who run competitively have a problem. However there is a higher prevalence of eating disorders in runners, athletes and professional ballerinas. And athletes tend to share possibly dangerous (or not) personality traits such as perfectionism, determination, self-motivation, and great pressure to be thin.[23]

♦ **Expert Opinion by Paula Radcliffe, Sports Personality, and the World Record Marathon Holder.**

Follow the good example set out by the success of Paula; this is her message to readers of this book, understanding that there will be people suffering from eating disorders, many of whom are obsessed with exercise. Her advice to athletes, sports enthusiasts, indeed, anyone not-eating properly, or thinking of not-eating properly and wanting to succeed:

> *"Getting the best out of your body and life requires fuelling your body with all that it requires to function optimally. In my sport I expect and ask a lot of my body; in return I look after it by eating well and healthily. I always try and eat foods high in carbohydrates and also including protein within 30mins of finishing exercise, as this is the optimum time to refuel. I also make sure to include enough vitamins and minerals and fresh fruit and veg, as well as the good fats etc. You wouldn't expect a car to run without fuel or on the wrong fuel so don't*

---

[23] Picard, C.L. (1999). *The level of competition as a factor for the development of eating disorders in female collegiate athletes.* Journal of Youth and Adolescence, 28, p. 583-594.

expect your body to manage. Failing to look after your body and to fuel it properly is a dangerous and foolish mistake. You only get one body so you should look after it and never abuse it."

☙ *Paula Radcliffe, 2nd October, 2005.*

○ **Treatments for Anorexia nervosa.**

If anorexia is suspected, a medical opinion is imperative. *The sooner it is treated, the greater the chance of recovery, and smaller the chance of serious complications – both mental and physical.* I cannot emphasise that point enough. Anorexia is now well recognised, but if you receive an unenthusiastic response, seek an urgent second opinion. Some people can afford private care. On the *NHS* in the UK, most people have to wait[24] a considerable time: even when extremely ill. Treatment Guidelines for anorexia are laid out in the 2004 NICE guidelines.[25]

Many people do not accept they are ill, or if they do, like I did, they don't believe they *deserve* help at all. A variety of treatments are available including medication

---

[24] Thus if this applies to you, seek help quickly and get on that waiting list. You can always turn down help when you do reach the top.
[25] NICE - National Institute of Clinical Excellence, National Health Service, UK.
Website: http://www.nice.org.uk/ See the (2004) *NICE guidelines for Eating disorders: Core interventions in the treatment and management of anorexia nervosa, bulimia nervosa and related eating disorders.*

for some, if say depressed, fulltime inpatient treatment centres, day centres, one to one therapy, or just weekly meetings. Paying for healthcare with or without insurance is an option for some people, in the UK, and in other countries. It is a very expensive problem. I was unable to afford to go privately, and against doing so in principle, regardless of my health (an emotionally dangerous principle, but my belief none the less). I have wasted over four years in total to get various outpatient therapies. There is something very wrong with the system of health care in the UK.

For anorectics of very low weight, at risk of suicide or with complex needs such as a dependency problem, inpatient care may be needed for safety but there are not nearly the necessary number of inpatient beds available, so people get more ill, suffer, and some die. Being underweight, and/or drinking, and/or self-harming, and/or being actively suicidal, will *not* guarantee you a bed. Starting to eat can have medical complications that are generally more life-threatening the more underweight the patient, and physical health must be closely monitored, especially during the first few days of re-feeding, when electrolyte imbalances (for example changes in the level of potassium in the blood, needed for a healthy, regular heart beat) can be fatal.

Because some people do not seek help, and/or because of long waits for treatment, some people unfortunately are extremely emaciated and very seriously ill by the time they receive help. It is well understood by anyone with insight into eating disorders that coercion to eat is *not* helpful in the long-term management of eating disorders, but in extreme cases where the patient will die without intervention; force can be used as a last resort. Several attempts have been made to challenge the right of doctors to make this decision against the express wishes of the patient, but the right to intervene has been upheld. Such force-feeding is should only be carried out in hospital by experts. Legally this is possible under the Mental Health Act 1983 or Children Act 1989.

Eating *always* has a psychological toll that requires professional support. (I have to say, I have always found such support unhelpful, and that it felt patronising in the short-term, but I know many who do not agree). Professionals should always be aware of the risk of suicide and self-harm. There are excellent treatment plans in existence these days: replacing the older fatten-up-and-kick-them-out units, although these still exist also. It still feels like the only important issue is gaining weight; a focus that I do not believe to be healthy. All health professionals place too much emphasis on weight, but I guess it is hard not to do so. I am not saying weight is unimportant; I am saying it is not as important as many people believe.

Some people are well enough for a middle-way approach, and attend day care treatment centres where they receive various therapies and undergo a daily meal regime. This is often in groups of sufferers, with supportive staff. Inpatient care may be combined with, or lead onto this type of day patient care.

Most people receive outpatient therapy/counselling. *Talking treatments* are the best way of treating eating disorders. Cognitive behavioural therapy (CBT) works; in particular to change core beliefs such as self-hatred, to understand why such eating disordered behaviour is "useful" to you (individually) in order to cope and to provide an experienced, warm human being who is prepared to help and accept *unconditionally* that you are valid and deserving human being, not some worthless, unspeakable monster. I say this because I have experienced it first hand. Therapy of any kind may be ongoing for some time irrespective of patient status. Unfortunately in some cases the therapist is limited to say eight sessions with a patient, not long to build trust and work on a complex problem.

There are many other forms of therapy, such as group therapy, dialectical behavioural therapy (DBT), psychodynamic therapy, cognitive analytic therapy (CAT), interpersonal psychotherapy (IPT) that a GP, psychiatrist and/or psychologist will recommend based on each individual case. Self-help organisations are valuable, in particular in the UK; the Eating Disorders Association now called "Beat." There are also some excellent websites. (See the information at the back of the book). Some people see school councillors, or talk to their GP. In children and adolescents, family involvement in treatment is important, as is individual care. All forms of therapy may be stopped if the patient does not improve: although this is not a rash decision, it is necessary due to the demand for help.

Care is needed not to substitute another problem (e.g. alcoholism, bulimia) for the anorexia – which unfortunately is quite a common occurrence. The anorectic must therefore learn strategies by which to cope with their life that do not do harm. Any concurrent illness, such as a mood disorder and/or alcoholism and/or the addiction to pills that are easy to get over the Internet/ etc., must also be treated, as these are likely to have been part of the cause of the anorexia, and are definitely reasons why the anorexia is *maintained*. Not treating the concurrent illness would probably lead to a relapse, the development of another eating disorder, or other serious psychiatric problems. For example, depression could become severe and lead to suicidal ideation or self-harming behaviour or alcoholism could become more severe.

Although anorexia nervosa is a psychiatric condition, physical health must be carefully monitored. This does not mean just weight, it means blood tests (particularly potassium levels in purging anorectics) and longer-term issues such as osteoporosis (low bone density) that can be treated with oestrogen in adult patients. Oestrogen should never be given to children or adolescents as it can cause premature fusion of the epiphyses.

- **Final Thought on Anorexia and Image.**

    "You are not a chicken," my therapist said. "What on Earth...?" I asked with incredulity. She replied, "I mean I don't value you based on your weight. Now a chicken in a supermarket is priced according to its weight. I don't value you by your weight. You are not a chicken!"

    ࿂ Real conversation in a therapy session with my Oxford psychotherapist.

I have misgivings that *all* anorectics fit the stereotypical diagnostic feature of seeing a fat person in the mirror. I do *not* dispute the fact that some sufferers do see a fat person in the mirror. Certainly all eating disorder sufferers can at times "see" themselves as fatter than they are, more often it is a *feeling*. I suspect that more sufferers *know and see* that they are underweight, possibly not how much (people will misjudge the gravity of their situation to varying degrees and on various days). For many anorectics, their low weight is a very evident, obvious statement to the world around them that they hurt, and something they are usually proud of.

As it is part of the diagnostic criteria, it is common for doctors and therapists to ask their anorectic patients, "Do you see yourself as fat when you look in the mirror." This is a leading question – yes or no? Of course, even without a guiding question, dichotomous thinking could lead to an all-or-nothing, fat-or-thin response, which is not entirely accurate. "Yes" is more correct than "no," but not a full answer. For most victims the actual answer is not a simple yes or no, rather "*more* fat than they would like, fatter, larger." That is very different from a simple response of "fat," which is the simple response given/heard. Also, anorectics are bright people, they will have read extensively on the topic of anorexia and may wish to have, or not have, a diagnosis, and will answer accordingly.

When I was being assessed (and wanted help), I lied, replying that I saw myself as fat because I knew they needed to hear that response to diagnose me. I was *never* in any delusion about how underweight/skeletal I became. I've asked every person I know with an eating disorder about this, and most admit to knowing they were thin, too thin, or even skeletal. That's the whole point! An addiction to liking feeling/appearing/being too thin, combined with many possible delusions: such as that punishment is deserved and (commonly) thinking everyone hates them and thinks them disgusting. It's this internal, poor self-image and valuing of self by thinness that needs addressing, not what is or is not seen in the mirror. That corrects itself (if, indeed it was ever wrong).

I do not deny that some people do see a fat person because it has been repeatedly stated so often that it must be true in some, maybe even most cases. I just think there are a lot of people out there who know they are underweight and can see it totally or to some extent feel it a lot of the time.

Chapter 2: Bulimia Nervosa.

> "Never in my life, have I hated myself more, than when the bulimia demon takes control, blasting aside my soothing anorexia. Suddenly I'm buying disgusting food I can't afford, forcing this food down a burning throat, not tasting it, filling a stomach until literally ready to burst. The guilt, the shame, the hours being sick, the tiredness this brings, the relief at the final wretch...only for the demon to start it all again. When it is over, my body is shaking and shattered, my heart beating rapidly in my throat; I fear my heart will burst. I think I might actually die. I lie there still, maybe if I don't move I will live. My mind is temporarily purged (note: *temporarily*). I hate this weakness of mine."

ત Katy Sara Culling, age 21, University of Nottingham Diary.

Bulimia nervosa is a cruel trap. What one day seems like a simple solution to eating a bit too much, or a desire to lose weight, which turns rapidly into a soul destroying, full-time obsession: reducing victims to suffer severe distress, self-disgust, anxiety, money problems, relationship problems, and the very real risk of death. Bulimics are highly emotional and susceptible to mood disorders like depression. Whereas the low-weight anorectic is typically (not always) more closed off and numb, sometimes appearing happy with their illness and weight loss, bulimics and purging-type anorectics tend to be people who need *immediate* gratification to order "cope" with intense feelings that they simply have no other recourse for.

The main reason why bulimia "works" for people is that is creates an absolute, obsessive focus on food, bingeing, purging, dieting, weight and control, which blocks other issues in life out. Bulimia is a form of oblivion, and a very effective one at that. This coping strategy is highly addictive psychologically and physically. Thus with or without an understanding of terrible negative complications, people become ensnared. Bulimics have an emotional "hole" that they fill temporarily with food. Ultimately it's a case of filling one hole with an even bigger hole.

A person with bulimia may be very underweight, normal weight, through to overweight or obese (rarely morbidly obese). It is typical to find a bulimic presenting for help within the normal weight range – this is because no matter how "good" a person becomes at purging, some energy/calories are absorbed, which is usually enough to keep the person from becoming emaciated or even particularly underweight. This, combined with secrecy due to intense shame, means bulimia nervosa is often far harder to spot than anorexia. The weight of a bulimic will fluctuate up and down quite severely within short periods of time – I remember one friend telling me she had gained 2kg (4.4lb) overnight – it was mostly fluid of course. At first weight may be lost, but soon this is regained as the urge to binge becomes uncontrollable.

Reflective Reflections

Bulimia means "Hunger of an Ox,"[26] which is rather derogatory. People with bulimia recurrently binge and then purge. Bingeing means "eating a large amount of food, far more than 'normal' in a discrete period of time, usually within two hours." Deciding if the amount eaten is normal (when really there is no such thing as 'normal') is based on what a 'normal' person would eat in a similar time and circumstances, and is therefore a subjective experience and/or description. This eating is accompanied by a sense of a lack of control around what and how much is eaten. To fit the diagnostic criteria for bulimia (as opposed to binge eating disorder), a bulimic will repeatedly take serious compensatory measures to remove the food and/or prevent weight gain, and the bingeing will tend to be more extreme (though of course, this varies). These "balancing" measures involve purging and non-purging methods. Non-purging methods include going for long periods without eating, exercising, some drugs and diet pills. Purging usually means self-induced vomiting, i.e. being sick, thus removing food from the bulimic's digestive system before it can be properly digested. Some alternative methods of purging are overuse of laxatives, diuretics, and enemas and in extreme cases, bloodletting. Sometimes more than one, or even all of these methods are used to control weight.

Bulimia has *very* serious health implications – immediate and long-term, life-threatening problems: physical and psychological, together with negative emotional, financial and relationship considerations. The sufferer is often aware of all this, but is trapped; one might even use the word "addicted." Common feelings are shame, disgust, fear, anxiety and loneliness, along

---

[26] Derived from the Greek *Bous* "ox", *Limos* "hunger," and Latin *Bulimus* (derived from the Greek).

with self-hatred for being uncontrollable, and guilt for feeling weak, as opposed to accepting that the illness is in control.

Unlike in anorexia, where the sufferer may remain in denial that they have a problem for some time, most bulimics cannot avoid the immediate realisation that their behaviour is self-destructive and 'wrong.' Resultant despair will habitually cause or worsen depression that is usually already present. Bingeing will temporarily alleviate this depression, which is one reason bingeing continues (maintenance factor); but after "failing" by bingeing yet again, the person feels even *more* depressed. Thus a vicious circle is established.

The **DSM-IV Criteria for Bulimia Nervosa**[27] are the world-standardised criteria used for diagnosis of mental disorders, although you may also find the **ICD-10** useful (For a comparison see[28]).

❖ **List of Diagnostic Symptoms of Bulimia Nervosa.**

> ❖ Binge eating, out of control, (eating more than might be considered normal in a set period of time) then followed by one or more

---

[27] Absolutely strict diagnostic criteria that are used by physicians worldwide are found in the DSM-IV *Diagnostic and Statistical Manual of Mental Disorders, Fourth Edition*, (1994). Copyright American Psychiatric Association. For Bulimia nervosa see p. 549-550.
[28] Classification of Eating Disorders (1995) *Classification and Diagnosis of Eating Disorders*. In: Brownell KD, Fairburn CG, (Eds). *Eating Disorders and Obesity: a comprehensive handbook*. New York: Guilford Press, 1995, p.125-134.

of the compensatory methods explained above (e.g. vomiting is the most popular). I.e. Out of control bingeing and a compensatory measure should *both* occur, at least two times a week for a period of three months. However if you are concerned, you do not have to wait that long to seek help.

❖ A bulimic will typically evaluate his or her own self-worth basing disproportionate importance on their own size, weight and shape, instead of other things such as being a good friend.

❖ The person is not already in an episode of anorexia nervosa. (In which case anorexia nervosa purging type is the diagnosis. A diagnosis of anorexia trumps a diagnosis of bulimia).

Amenorrhea (cessation of menstruation) is not a requirement for a diagnosis of bulimia nervosa, although up to 50% of sufferers experience partial or complete amenorrhea as a result of being low weight and/or stress.

A binge consists of eating, for some people, massive volumes of food and put the person at risk of immediate death for a variety of reasons – e.g. their stomachs could rupture.

As mentioned, bulimics are split into purging type and non-purging type. The word purging used in this was is defined as "the act of clearing yourself, or an act of removing by cleansing: i.e. ridding yourself of undesired elements – food/ calories/ kilojoules/ fat/ carbohydrate/ bulk – and emotions that are strangely, yet closely linked to all of these food issues and behaviours. Bulimia is then further specified into purging or non-purging type.

Specify type:

❖ *Non-purging type.* A form of bulimia whereby the sufferer does not engage in vomiting, laxatives, diuretics, or enemas after binge eating. Instead long fasts or exercise may be used alone, to counteract the binge. (But this is painful – not "just" like oops eating too much at Thanksgiving or Christmas), but less is consumed than for purging type bulimics who may eat till they can hardly walk.

❖ *Purging type.* These poor sufferers use every means at their disposal to prevent weight gain following binge eating with purging, and the most common method used is vomiting. Laxatives, diuretics, enemas, emetics, might also be used. Non-purging methods such as exercise, drugs, and strict-dieting/fasting may be used as well. Very large amounts of food can be consumed when a person knows they are going to vomit afterwards. You think to yourself, well if I'm going to be sick I may as well eat a bit more whilst I'm at it. In extreme cases 30,000kcals or more could be consumed in one binge. (Baring in mind the usual daily intake for a woman is 2,000kcals, and 2,500kcals for men).

Bingeing is expensive: avoid bulimia!

Purging and non-purging methods may be applied concurrently; indeed purging and non-purging methods are usually employed in a controlled yet haphazard fashion: resulting in a far more hectic, out-out-control form of illness than anorexia.

All forms of purging are more *ineffectual* at controlling weight than is realised by the disorder's victim believes, although this will vary from person to person, and depend on technique and "expertise." I must have been very good at vomiting because I endured huge binges and then long periods (hours) vomiting until it was impossible to get anything more out. But had I not binged at all my weight would have gone even lower. Some other methods are totally ineffective with respect to preventing weight gain, keeping in control, and there is a risk an instant or slow death.

You might suddenly find you are spending a disproportionate amount of time with you head down the toilet. I remember the years passing me by like this, in a whirlwind of chaos, celebrating each New Year at midnight, kneeling on the bathroom floor, holding my hair back, and, well... making myself sick. As I mentioned, I must have been quite good at it because I maintained a very low weight for my height. The lowest I got my BMI down to was 13 whilst bingeing and purging.

♠ Figure 1: The vicious circle of non-control in Bulimia Nervosa (and Anorectic Bulimia).

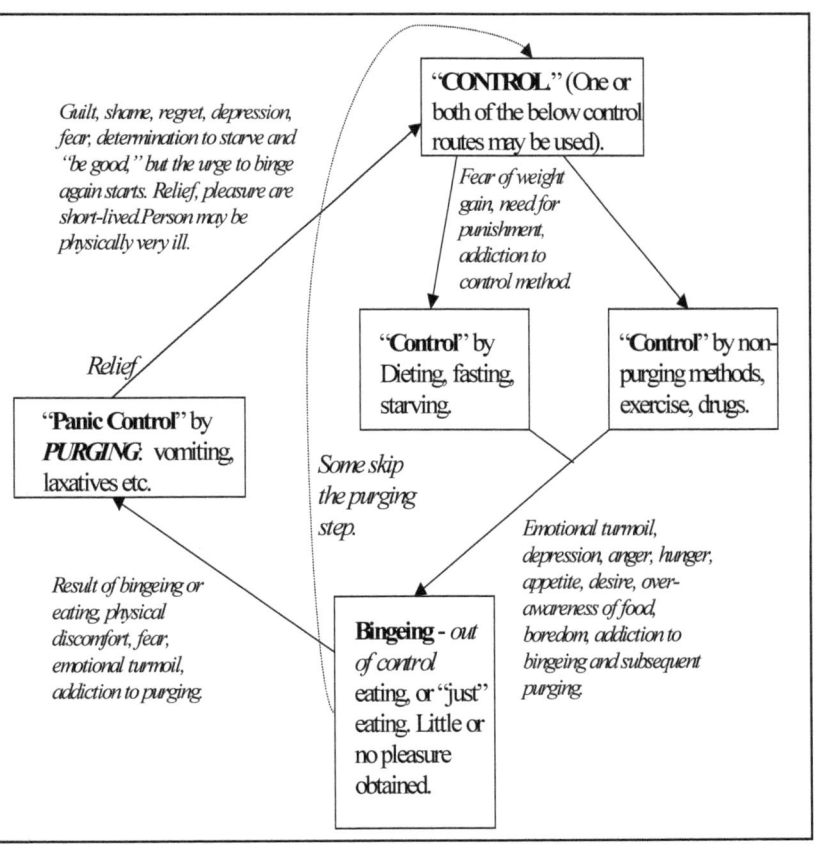

Reflective Reflections

o **Predisposing, precipitating and maintaining factors.**

Predisposing factors for eating disorders have already been discussed in some detail, and all can apply to bulimia nervosa. A mixture of nature and nurture lead to the development of bulimia as a coping strategy for life. Up to 60% of bulimics are former anorectics – with an all-or-nothing approach still being taken towards food. All bulimics are trying to control their weight, with normal-dieting a common precipitating factor. Some become bulimic by starting to purge after eating normally: because of fears about weight and appearance, and ultimately end up bingeing. Some people become bulimic induced by an uncontrollable urge to binge on food for comfort, after which they then start to compensate. This ends up dominating the life of a bulimic. Ultimately the compulsion to binge and compensate are terrifically powerful and massively destructive.

You may start by being sick once, and then occasionally after eating more than you would like. Fairly quickly this will turn into physical and psychological cravings, and you start to think: *Well, if I'm going to eat and purge, I may as well make the most of it and eat more of the things I am craving... More food, more naughty food... Yes, this is "wonderful," I can eat anything bad, and then undo what I have done.* Eating converts into bingeing on anything and everything; and fairly soon, the compulsive desire to binge more and more often becomes paramount in life – from a few times a week up to often several times a day. At my worst I did it three times a day, seven days a week. The absolute and urgent need to purge is usually a no-brainer decision once a binge has taken place; indeed it is usually already a set-in-stone decision prior to food starting to pass the lips of a sufferer.

Vomiting intentionally, just once, can quickly or immediately hook you into repeating the behaviour: effectually becoming addicted to vomiting unable to predict or control your behaviour. In other words, the *need* to vomit (or purge in other ways) can be as important as the need to binge beforehand, although most people see the need to binge as the driving force. The relief felt following purging is immense and better than any drug. Although like crack cocaine, the pleasant sensations are extremely short-term, tolerance and craving build quickly. Thus the bulimia is maintained and/or worsened. I was addicted to vomiting – I hated myself and felt I deserved the punishment. I also got off on being good at it, and because I was concentrating on it so hard I achieved a form of oblivion from all the other issues in my life - numbness. I hated it at the same time though, the best part of any day for me was the moment when I'd just finished vomiting and I knew it was over, at least until tomorrow.

Other maintaining factors include concurrent psychiatric illness, commonly mood disorders and/or alcoholism, low self-esteem, and risky behaviours (sex, self-harm etc.) Bulimics usually have serious and painful problems with which they have no way to cope. And so bulimia fills that gap, blanking out all other concerns: hence bulimia is in effect a symptom of other deeper issues. Soon food, bingeing, vomiting/purging are all that exist in life – and that can be a very powerful anaesthetic to aid forgetfulness of other problems in life. Of course, it solves nothing and only adds to the battle for survival. Family, friendships, work, and health all suffer – only adding to the problems in life that cannot be coped with, compounding the problem more and more the longer it persists. Although bulimia may immediately distract someone from a low mood: overall, this relief is slight, temporary, depression tends to deepen, and self-esteem plummets – all of this irrespective of weight change.

Once vomiting becomes second nature, it is very hard to psychologically cope with keeping food down properly. Indeed gastric emptying is slowed, and food in the stomach soon feels uncomfortable – whether following "normal" eating, under-eating, or a binge. The psychological need for a source of powerful oblivion is a major maintaining factor that no pill can treat.

What a bulimic eats in between vomiting sessions can affect whether they binge and vomit/purge. Someone trying to starve is more likely to snap and binge, than someone eating regularly. Hunger can therefore be a maintaining factor – and so bulimics must learn to eat little and often. To recover it is not possible to just eliminate food from your life (like a heroin user might do with heroin). No: you have to learn to eat little and often, you have to learn real control – this can be hard when what constitutes a normal portion has become unknown to the bulimic.

However it is important to note that feeling physically hungry is a far less important trigger than emotional turmoil.

o **Delving a little deeper into the behaviours in Bulimia nervosa: warning signs.**

Many of the obsessive food behaviours found in anorexia nervosa can also be found in people with bulimia. It is always a very individual problem: a unique mixture of issues, with a lot of overlap. Those behaviours already covered earlier in this book will not be repeated here; instead we shall focus on methods of bingeing and purging.

When I was most ill with anorexia nervosa, purging type, (or anorectic bulimia), I used five purging/non-purging methods concurrently. Vomiting was by far the most important and effective method of purging for me. It is also the most common method used by people with purging type bulimia. This is *not* a recommendation to vomit, as you risk death from the very first time you try it, and will quickly become very ill. For me it was about seeking oblivion and punishing myself.

It is worth remembering that sometimes the need to purge (to punish, and/or for distraction) may be the subconscious raison d'être – although it is *usually* a less appealing part of the process. Both the mental clearing of unwanted emotions, the physical cleansing of food energy (joules, calories) and the physical bulk of food from the body apply. Vomiting is a violent, yet highly effective way of purging yourself of unwanted feelings and emotions although a bulimic can be completely unaware, at a conscious level, of the mental cleansing that physically purging "rewards" them. I was oblivious: I just knew it felt good as well as bad.

Bulimics may or may not eat "normally" in between binges, but irrespective of this, weight is likely to be very difficult to control and to shift markedly even within a day. People can *gain* weight because they think they have managed to get rid of all the fattening food that they binged on, whereas they have not.

Laxatives and diuretics are also used for purging purposes, and nowadays people seem keen to use enemas and treatments such a colonic irrigation to cleanse themselves. Some people take the cleansing to an extreme and clean themselves, their insides, outsides, home, indeed anything to excess. Laxatives and diuretics can be bought over the counter in any chemist shop.

In the UK it is not possible to buy syrup of Ipecac – an emetic that can be bought over the counter in America, intended for *one* time use in accidental poisoning. It's not hard to see how this substance appeals to someone purging – someone desperate – turning to a poison for relief. A small amount causes vomiting, but excessive use, i.e. repeated usage over time and/or an excessive dose on any one occasion: *kills*. The alkaloid emetine from the Ipecac syrup causes severe damage to the heart muscle – which can cause death or illness, both immediately or long after recovery.

It is unclear if using bloodletting fits best into purging or non-purging type. For myself personally, bloodletting was never about purging, but for others, it is. Bloodletting is purgative where people do it under the miscomprehension that they are literally leeching out calories in their blood, and the glucose or fats contained in it. In actual fact, blood loss slows the metabolism, and may even result in weight gain.

There are many bogus (expensive) weight loss pills – and some that are illegal or prescription only, that can aid weight loss but that have potentially serious side effects. Some drugs used effectively as a weight loss medication for genuinely overweight people, such as Orlistat, especially if abused, are purgative because of the mechanism of action of the drug. Orlistat prevents fat digestion, which therefore has to be excreted, and, well, there's only one place for it to go – and it's not pretty. Street drugs such as Amphetamine (speed) and cocaine do aid weight loss but are rather illegal.

All of these purgative methods are *intended* to remove, reduce or balance the food that the bulimic has consumed during the binge. And as I will point out later, none of them are totally efficient and indeed some are totally useless.

Nowadays there is so much in the media and peer groups about bulimia, self-induced vomiting is not a difficult idea for someone desperately worrying about their weight to consider. Occasionally someone will be taught how to binge and/or vomit by someone else, especially amongst female students and fellow eating disordered victims. I learned the most about ways to harm myself the first time I received hospital treatment, and was able to spend time talking to other eating disorder patients. Some people binge and vomit in groups, although to me, shame meant it was a private act. There are stories of acid from vomit destroying pipes in school bathrooms, or flooding sewage systems though I am sceptical.

You cannot cure bulimia by physically restraining anyone, or similar macho acts. They will find ways to binge and vomit somehow. I know a well-intentioned father who removed the door from the bathroom to prevent his daughter vomiting, so she threw up in carrier bags, the dustbin or public toilets.

The act of vomiting gives many signs that a friend, family member or doctor can pick up on. If you think you are getting away with it unnoticed, you almost certainly are *not*. People notice if food goes missing, or you eat massive quantities and do not gain lots of weight, or you actually lose weight. Although weight changes (or lack thereof) are less evident than in anorexia: they are still noticeable.

Quite often, a bulimic is "good" at hiding the act of vomiting, although it is likely that those close to her realise what she is doing. The victim and those close might maintain denial about this fact, or not care, or feel hopeless to challenge or change what is happening. Signs such as getting up from the dinner table and rushing to the bathroom are obvious. But also consider people turning on bath or shower water to muffle the sound of vomiting. Some people appear to take several showers or baths in the day, when really purging. There is often a regular pattern to such purging, and therefore regularly "having a shower," at possibly unusual times. Other signs include the slight smell of vomit, or possibly the smell of soap, cleaner, bleach or deodorising room spray in an attempt to hide the smell of vomit. The bulimic may very well clean the toilet/sink and walls of the bathroom: cleanliness is a warning sign, one often missed. Vomit on the carpet is particularly difficult to clean; hence some bulimics will cover the carpet with towels or plastic bags to protect themselves from detection. All these things I did. Aside from the bathroom, the bulimic may throw up in bins, carrier bags, nearby shops, ally ways, indeed anywhere. These are harder to spot for the family/friends/flat-mates.

However there are many other signs that someone is tortured by bulimia. Mood swings are terrible – the agitation surrounding food, bingeing, eating, purging is extreme and everyone involved feels like they are walking on eggshells. Bite marks: callosities, abrasions or scars (Russell's sign) on the knuckles of the hand can be seen, caused by repeated stimulation of the gag reflex with fingers and hands, and thus catching the hand on teeth. Cold sores around the mouth are common; healing is slow because they are repeatedly cracked open when vomiting.

Dental problems are almost omnipresent, with erosion of enamel, particularly the lingual surface, due to both bingeing on high-sugar foods and the acid in the vomit when brought back up. Any dentist will spot the signs, even if she or he remains quiet. Bulimia might result in crowns or dentures, fillings, rotten teeth, pain, dental bills – for life. I didn't believe that when I was younger but trust me, I now know it is very true.

Advice if you do vomit: do not brush your teeth after vomiting, as this brushes the acid harder into your teeth, doing more damage. If you feel able, drink some milk, unless that would start another binge. Otherwise rinse your mouth with milk or lots of water; brush your teeth later and use a fluoride containing mouthwash.

For anything from minutes to hours after the act of vomiting the eyes will be puffy and red. For a matter or days after vomiting the parotid and submandibular glands will be swollen, easily spotted if you know what you are looking for. The parotid glands are at each side of the face, just in front and level with the ears. When these swell the face looks wider than usual. This wide face can be taken as further "evidence" to the bulimic or purging-type anorectic that she is too fat, and should lose weight. Sometimes only one gland swells leading to an asymmetric swelling of the face. The submandibular glands are in the lower throat and neck, and again swell. Swelling of these glands can last for many hours, or days, especially after repeated violent vomiting: all obvious symbols of bulimia to a knowing eye. Teeth marks on the fingers and hand area dead give away. All signs of the brutality being done to the victim's body by the vomiting, but not nearly the whole story of the damage being done internally.

Vomiting is often thought of as being a good way of voiding the body of calories. Actually it is not always very efficient, though it depends on each person's ability, learned "expertise," and methods. Average suggestions are that 40% of what you binge upon is retained in the body; upper estimates are that 70% is digested. These figures have been discussed amongst bulimic patients and myself: knowing how much was really eaten on binges, what happened to our weight, the consensus was that there is *no way* such high percentages of food energy from bingeing were being retained. However, many bulimics *lose* weight when they stop bingeing, which would suggest that for most people, the amount of food actually absorbed is far higher than they would like us to believe. I would estimate that anything from 10% is digested but that "good" bulimics can get rid of 70%, 80% or even 90% via vomiting. Some may only get rid of 40% as a random number picked out of the air.

Some people retain a greater percentage of calories than others. Some food is *always* retained and digested: proven by the fact that restricting anorectics tend to get much thinner, much quicker than purging-type anorectics or bulimics. Obviously those bulimics who eat normally some of the time, will be a more normal weight than bulimics who alternatively starve and binge, though if the said bulimic is not very efficient at vomiting, she may be a normal, or high weight. Basically, a bulimic can be practically *any* weight depending on how "well" she vomits, and what she eats in between binges.

So how do you vomit/purge efficiently I almost hear those bulimics amongst you curiously ask: desperate for tips to improve your method? To tell you specifics would be highly irresponsible. However, I will discuss some very well known methods.

Firstly, there are the features of the binge that will make subsequent vomiting easier later. Something you learn very quickly is what food to eat that you find easy to subsequently vomit. I couldn't vomit potato or bread, but I know others who thought these were easy. If I wanted to eat something I knew I couldn't throw up, I'd eat peas. I just couldn't vomit peas! It's an individual thing. In general, liquid and soft foods are most people's choice, pasta in sauces, ice cream and so on. Large quantities of liquid are needed. Some people use carbonated drinks in the belief that this make food float at the top of the stomach... well, let's just say they are wrong. The least dense substance, i.e. the air, will remain at the top of the stomach.

Some people start their binge by swallowing something to decrease their gastric emptying rate, thus keeping food in the stomach and decreasing absorption of food before they can throw it up. I am not disclosing that one, and it is not very common. The only girl/woman I knew who did that, was a four stone bulimic. It's usual for a bulimic to be so low in weight. Her life was exceptionally unsustainable; she is now dead.

Most binges last longer than half an hour, and might last up to around two hours. Glucose (sugar) immediately begins to be absorbed, and will start to peak in the bloodstream within fifteen minutes, protein digestion is slower but continuous, and fat digestion is slowest. What I am basically saying is, the longer your binge, the longer the time you body has to absorb calories; but whatever you do, the body latches on to them quickly.

Reflective Reflections

It is quite common to start a binge with a marker food, red pepper, beetroot, or tomato: something that can easily be spotted on its way back up, so that you know (think) you have got rid of all the food. This is a mistake, because food gets mixed up quite well, quite quickly, and therefore you might see your marker food whilst there is still plenty of food down there. Some people start their binge with safer foods that they think of as lining their stomach, hence not being too bad if they are absorbed, (lower calorie, lower fat, lower carb, high fibre), and eat the more "bad" foods towards the end of the binge. I did that.

As for actual induction of emesis: I wish to avoid listing many various techniques. The method of sticking two or three fingers (or a hand) down the throat is commonplace. This usually scratches and damages the throat. The other famous method is sticking a toothbrush down your throat to achieve the same effect on the gag reflex. Never worked for me. Toothbrushes or spoons reach further down your throat, which can seriously damage the back of the throat. People tend to develop their own safe-feeling technique.

There are ways of positioning that reduce the strain put on the body: stand (not kneeling) with your legs straight, so that your stomach can contract fully, and the vomit is more or less coming down hill. Note that this reduces the strain on the body; it does *not* eliminate it: the strain *and danger* is still considerable.

Cutting down the times vomited, and/or resting for periods in between vomiting-days gives muscles time to recover from the ordeal, whereas if it is a daily or several times daily event, muscles are tired and the gag reflex dulled: in other words, the efficiency of vomiting can be reduced. This is not true for everyone, some people get better and better with practice. Some people are even able to vomit spontaneously by bending over the toilet.

Psychology soon begins to play a role in vomiting/purging; this is due to anxiety of the victim to maintain weight loss or not gain weight. A couple of well known techniques are to vomit a certain number of times, or take a certain number of laxatives, those numbers feeling safe, though the "safe" number will often creep upwards, similar to obsessive compulsive disorder (OCD). Some people vomit (or use laxatives to achieve) a measured volume excreted. Some use weighing scales to make sure their weight before bingeing is the same as their weight after. The other technique being to be sick, drink water, be sick, drink water and so on, until the returning emesis becomes clear: known as *the wash-out method*. I did this. Some people have short waiting periods to allow the water they drink in between vomiting to mix properly with any remaining food in their stomach. Once the returning vomit reaches a satisfactory clarity, the exhausted person will stop. Food and feelings purged. Sometimes they then start all over again. This is highly dangerous.

Please note that this *washout method*, whilst common, is very dangerous because it can cause hypokalaemia, (low blood potassium – an electrolyte in the blood, important for muscle contraction and nerve conduction), which can cause a heart attack. After the binge you can be left shaking, sweaty and ill feeling, partly from the exhaustion, partly from tricking your body into releasing insulin that is not needed, and partly because of altered electrolytes. Laxative and/or diuretic abuse can also cause electrolyte imbalances, which can be fatal: as you might expect, using more than one technique is more dangerous than using only one.

Reflective Reflections

Many a bulimic has been found dead kneeling at a toilet, through heart failure, because of the massive strain vomiting puts on the heart, and plummeting blood potassium levels. Some also die from stomach or oesophageal rupture and blood loss. Even people who realise they are ruptured can be too afraid and ashamed to seek medical advice. If you are vomiting blood, (or losing it rectally when abusing laxatives) seek medical attention *immediately*.

Laxatives work on the large bowel, expelling whatever is in the bowel along with water. Food is digested and absorbed in the stomach and small intestine, far before the laxative takes action. This basically means that laxative will have a minimal effect on you absorbing calories from food. They do not particularly aid weight loss, other than water-weight. Short-term problems of laxative abuse range from severe pain and extreme embarrassment, to death. Overuse, (using more than the recommended dose, especially for a prolonged time), particularly *stimulant* laxatives (senna, sennosides, bisacodyl) makes the bowel atonic (lazy). This causes constipation, and therefore the sufferer uses more laxative, in effect becoming physically dependent on laxatives. Packets of laxatives may be used in one day. A large dose might make you pleased because of a drop in weight, *but it is not real weight*, your fat levels will remain untouched. However you will be dehydrated, which can be very dangerous.

Just as vomiting can upset your electrolyte balance (especially lowering blood potassium), so can abusing laxatives. This imbalance can lead to shaking, chills, spasms, muscle cramps and anxiety about these frightening symptoms, especially if the sufferer is aware it could be fatal. Use of laxatives and enemas also increased the risk of infection to the colon, as the usual protective mucus is stripped away. There is also suggestion of a link to colon cancer. What might not damage you or someone else on one day might damage or kill you at any point.

Dehydration can cause headaches, blurry vision, weakness, fainting, shaking, kidney damage and death. Severe cases of dehydration will require emergency intravenous fluids as drinking may not hydrate cells quickly enough. When you drink fluids, your weight will return to what it was pre-laxatives. Many people with eating disorders restrict the fluid they drink, and choose to drink caffeinated drinks (coffee, cola, tea), which causes further dehydration, as does alcohol. Caffeine is a diuretic, causing overall water loss. Thus many people are living in a state of constant semi-dehydration.

Where there are electrolyte imbalances: oedema, particularly of the feet, is sometimes found. When someone forces their body into dehydration, the body responds by holding on to some extra water when it gets chance, which can add to the vicious cycle of laxative abuse, diuretics and vomiting. This retention of fluid causes a temporary weight gain, which can be very distressing for the victim, and possibly trigger even more bingeing, and more desperate purging. Anyone who purges should have regular blood tests to check their electrolyte levels (in the very least). Note that people on certain medications that might alter fluid levels (e.g. Lithium) or alter potassium concentrations (e.g. some antihypertensives) are at increased risk and need closer monitoring.

Gastric dilatation, (stretched, or distended stomach), is an emergency condition caused by bingeing, and which can result in a rupture. Everybody has a different stomach; there is no way to predict how quickly this life-threatening condition will be brought on. Nor is it safe to think: *Well, I binged on this amount before; it wont hurt me*. It could kill you. Remember that the victim (particularly an anorectic who purges) may have a shrunken stomach due to starvation – and so gastric dilatation quickly becomes a serious life-threatening event. The most common symptom is abdominal pain after ingestion of a meal, especially a large meal or binge. The person would feel heavy after eating, and might experience heartburn. (Symptoms found after eating in nearly every person recovering from an eating disorder). It is the extent of the pain, fear and amount of food compared to normal that must be considered. Blood in vomitus is a reason to go straight to the Emergency Department for help.

Most people with eating disorders are expert enough to know when something is wrong – and most are too ashamed to seek help. Dilatation can be treated conservatively, by safely inducing emesis in hospital, if the patient seeks help early enough. If the gastric dilatation progresses, the stomach loses its contractility, resulting in venous occlusion, infarction, and gastric perforation (a breech in the stomach wall) that leaks the stomach contents into the chest, which is almost always lethal. Surgeons could *attempt* to clean out the chest cavity, but this is difficult to do, and infection is common. Then the tear must be repaired – and this injury must be allowed a long time to heal – without any bingeing. A long and complicated hospital stay may be needed, probably on a surgical ward, not a ward that is particularly informed or sensitive to people with eating disorders.

Occasionally, even an experienced bulimic will binge, and then find herself unable to vomit: with no warning. They drink more water to help but nothing works; the stomach is stretched further, the food stays down, even after hours spent trying to vomit. This happened to me four or five times, and each was horrendous and terrifying; I sought no help as I was far too ashamed, I gave up when I was so tired, I could no longer move. Then I lay motionless, until I could start trying to vomit all over again. In each case I did eventually vomit but it took 4 or so hours.

A possible cause for this unable-to-vomit state is a trapped nerve near the pyloric sphincter of the stomach: preventing the usual gag reflex from inducing emesis. The nerve is trapped due to the pressure of the overfull stomach pressing on it. Do not drink more fluid if this happens, you risk rupturing your stomach, and actually make it harder to ultimately vomit – if you are unable to seek medical assistance, the best thing to do is lie down on your left side and wait. The warning message is: if you are going to binge, take care not to over do it. Ideally you would seek medical help to prevent rupture, long-term hospital stay or loss of life.

Be warned, *bingeing can kill in one session*, as happened to an anorexic bulimic model on her first binge. A 23-year-old model, starved herself down to 84lbs, died in London after gaining 19lb during one binge. This is an example of a massive binge, not advice that it is OK the binge less than she did. According to a letter in the British Medical Journal and the Lancet, the woman's fatal intake consisted of liver, kidneys, steaks, eggs, cheese, bread, mushrooms, carrots, a whole cauliflower, 10 peaches, 4 pears, 2 apples, 4 bananas, 2lbs of grapes and 2 glasses of milk.

Many people fall in to this trap of filling themselves with food to fill up some kind of gap or hole that they perceive within themselves. It is a behaviour that is very difficult to stop, and the gap, the yearning for fulfilment is never satisfied by bulimia. Just remember, every single time you binge or vomit, you could die. Bulimia also carries with it a risk of deliberate self-harm and suicide.

- **Treatments for bulimia nervosa.**

As in anorexia, the sooner treatment is sought for bulimia, the greater the chance of recovery and the smaller the risk to short/long-term psychological and physical health. Once the starve/binge/vomit cycle becomes "normal," it is notoriously hard to break. Bulimia is not something you will recover from without trying over and over again, and professional help is needed. All you can do is your best, and if that means being sick twice a day instead of three times, that is success not failure. If you don't manage to reduced your number of binges that is still success because at least you didn't binge even more. Bulimia will cling to you like the parasite that it is, wanting you to feed it with food, *but it can be beaten*. Perhaps sufferers wont believe me – one day, you *will* look back, and you will wonder how on Earth you managed to put yourself through such a living nightmare. Recovery will take time: months or years, depending on how long you have been ill. There will be setbacks, for which self-punishment and blame is not helpful, self-acceptance is vital.

Being powerless to control illness is not the same as not taking responsibility or not trying. You can't magically recover when you want, but you, and only you can take responsibility to choose whether to fight or give up. You are not failing, even if you are bingeing and purging, as long as you are honestly fighting. But a word of caution, do not allow this suggested self-kindness to trick you into staying ill, and not *really* fighting. If you do, it is only yourself that you are cheating.

Treatments for bulimia are the same as those already described for anorexia: namely talking treatments individually or in a group, including CBT, or even CBT-BN, a form of CBT especially developed for bulimia, DBT or another form of psychotherapy. Most patients are treated on an outpatient basis, indeed bulimics are less likely to be admitted to hospital unless complex needs present such as being very low weight, concomitant alcoholism or drug use, low mood, and/or suicidal ideation. Again, pressure on beds or the cost of treatment may prevent the care that is needed from being provided. (See the NICE guidelines).[29]

There has been some success treating bulimia with high dose (60mg) of Fluoxetine HCl (Prozac) daily, and indeed this is often the first line of treatment as it can be started as soon as help is sought from your general practitioner, whereas talking treatments usually involve a long waiting list. This may be because of the action of the drug lowering appetite but it is ineffectual for many sufferers. For me it did nothing.

One area many bulimics (and purging anorectics) feel hopeless about is that they can never return to normal bodily function after using laxatives, sometimes in massive doses for many years. The answer is, the human body is remarkable in how well it can recover in many cases: but it takes a little time. Ideally you should

---

[29] NICE (National Institute of Clinical Excellence, National Health Service, UK).
Website: http://www.nice.org.uk/ See (2004) *NICE guidelines for Eating disorders: Core interventions in the treatment and management of anorexia nervosa, bulimia nervosa and related eating disorders.*

Reflective Reflections

speak with a doctor who can help you through this process, but as many of you will be too embarrassed, here is some basic advice.

If you are using a small dose of laxatives, it is safe to stop and go "cold turkey." If you are using large numbers of laxatives, you may prefer to cut down day by day, and this would be my recommendation. Stopping laxative use/abuse causes rebound constipation, weight fluctuations and bloating, which are difficult problems for people with eating disorders to cope with. Eating a low-sodium (low-salt) diet can help reduce water retention. Try to remember that these symptoms are short-term, weight gain is not fat, just water, and the bloating will go.

Rebound constipation can be mild to severe, depending on the severity of your problem, and how easy it is for you to follow the recommendations below. But it does pass. To help, it is important to drink plenty of water (1-2 litres a day), even though you feel bloated, because lack of water will cause constipation. Eat plenty of fruit, but do not suddenly overdo it on fibre breakfast cereals. Physical withdrawal can take up to a month, but the psychological addiction can last much longer. For many people however, the return to usual bowel functioning is quicker. Whenever this happens, (i.e. after a short or long time) it is a huge relief and extremely pleasing, usually relieving psychological cravings, indeed it is a huge incentive never to use laxatives ever again.

Sometimes, severe, prolonged use means that the body is unable to recover from laxative or enema abuse. The body becomes dependent on laxatives to stimulate bowel movements, and enemas can stretch the colon, meaning its muscle tone is not good enough to push waste matter through. The choice to remain on laxatives should only be a decision made with a doctor's advice. You may recover after fifteen years of abuse; you may not recover after a year of abuse.

Again, care is needed not to substitute another problem (e.g. alcoholism, anorexia, B.E.D.) for the bulimia. A bulimic must learn other, less harmful tactics by which to cope with her or his life so as not to relapse. As with anorexia, any concurrent illness must be treated as an important part of the pathology (precipitating and maintaining factors) and must therefore be part of the recovery strategy.

Chapter 3: E.D.N.O.S. Eating Disorder Not Otherwise Specified.

"How soon my sorrow hath destroyed my face"

૱William Shakespeare (1564-1616)

This eating disorder classification, which *is* a formal psychiatric diagnosis, was designed to cover the huge number of people with pathologically disordered eating, but who do not fit into the neat and tidy criteria of anorexia or bulimia: *but still need help*. In other words, it is a diagnosis that is intended to be more flexible about providing health care for these very complex and unique-in-every-case problems. E.D.N.O.S. is sometimes referred to as an "**atypical**" eating disorder, and is often grouped into those people who have an illness that resembles anorexia nervosa, and those whose illness resembles bulimia nervosa.[30]

Predisposing and maintaining factors are the same as for other eating disorders. Generally the treatments are the same as for anorexia and bulimia, talking treatments, dietary advice, treatment of concurrent illness, an individual care plan best devised between the victim and her/his doctor and/or therapist. Concurrent psychiatric problems (mood disorders) and risk factors (self-harm, suicidal ideation) are almost universal.

---

[30] Fairburn C.G., Walsh B.T., (1995) *Atypical Eating Disorders*. In: Brownell KD, Fairburn CG, (Eds). *Eating Disorders and Obesity: a comprehensive handbook*. New York: Guilford Press, 1995, p.135-139.

The **DSM-IV Criteria**[31] are the world-standardised criteria used for diagnosis of mental disorders.

List of Diagnostic Symptoms of E.D.N.O.S.

Examples include:

❖ For females, all of the criteria for anorexia nervosa are met except that the individual does not have amenorrhea.

❖ All the criteria for anorexia nervosa are met except that, despite significant weight loss, the individual's weight is normal.

❖ All of the criteria for bulimia nervosa are met except that the bingeing and purging/compensatory mechanisms occur less than twice a week, or have not been present for the duration of 3 months or more.

❖ The regular use of inappropriate compensatory behaviour by a normal-weight individual, after eating small amounts of food (e.g., self-induced vomiting or using laxatives after the consumption of something "bad," like a bar of chocolate, in other words, *not* a binge).

---

[31] Absolutely strict diagnostic criteria that are used by physicians worldwide are found in the DSM-IV *Diagnostic and Statistical Manual of Mental Disorders, Fourth Edition*, (1994). Copyright American Psychiatric Association. For E.D.N.O.S. see p. 550.

Reflective Reflections

❖ Repeatedly chewing and spitting out various amounts of food, (usually large amounts), without swallowing.

❖ Bingeing without subsequent compensatory measures that are typical of bulimia nervosa.

Chapter 4 Compulsive Over Eating and Binge Eating Disorder.

> "Appetite grows keener by indulgence and all we can gratify it with at present serves but the more to inflame its insatiable desires."

≈ Benjamin Franklin (1706-1790)

Compulsive overeating (C.O.E.) and binge eating disorder (B.E.D.) are very serious conditions are very serious, valid, common problems, with significant co-morbidity issues. Compulsive over eating refers to eating significantly more than is needed over the day, usually by continually picking at food, for comfort, out of boredom etc. It is not a formal psychiatric diagnosis.

B.E.D. is a formal psychiatric diagnosis, which is essentially like bulimia nervosa without any or many of the characteristic, compensatory methods to control weight. (Technically it is a forum of E.D.N.O.S.)[32]

---

[32] Fairburn C.G., Walsh B.T., (1995) *Atypical Eating Disorders*. In: Brownell KD, Fairburn CG, (Eds). *Eating Disorders and Obesity: a comprehensive handbook*. New York: Guilford Press, 1995, p.137-139.

♠ Figure 2: The vicious circle of feelings and bingeing in B.E.D.

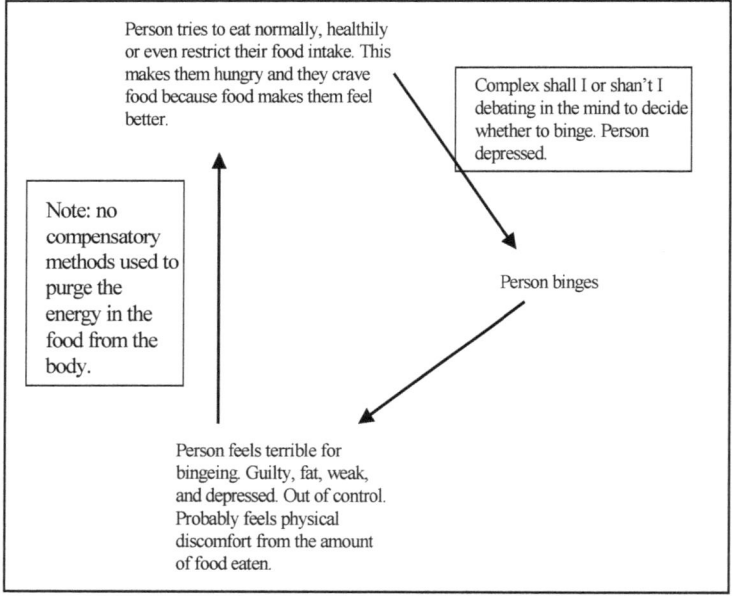

Unfortunately it is not always recognised as being as serious as it is. In fact it is a serious, life-threatening condition due to associated obesity, associated mood disorders and suicidal ideation. Unlike in anorexia and even bulimia the person is extremely aware of their situation and severe depression is likely. It treated in the same way as anorexia and bulimia, mainly by use of talking treatments, dietary advice, and treatment of concurrent illnesses, with care to remember that it is fairly common for people with one eating disorder to switch to another. CBT-BED may be offered, which is a specialised form of CBT for B.E.D.

C.O.E. AND B.E.D. can be associated strongly with mood disorders; in fact it is rare to find a sufferer who is not depressed and eating for comfort. It is important for professionals to recognise this and treat the depression very seriously. Otherwise, as with bulimia the person feels low in mood, eats to raise their mood, then feels terrible afterwards, and a vicious circle presents. Antidepressants are probably indicated; hopefully ones that don't cause weight gain.

Chapter 5: Thinking Cap On With Respect To Eating Disorders.

"A thought, even a possibility, can shatter and transform us"

≈ Friedrich Nietzsche

All eating disorders could really be considered different manifestations of one and the same illness: with the same drives, same problems, same fears, and the same utter self-hatred and disgust. Food is the enemy. The differences between someone who is anorectic, someone who is bulimic, and someone with B.E.D, are the disordered methods by which they deal with their illness – and there is often a great deal of overlap between the illnesses, between individuals, and over time. The differences are their symptoms, not the underlying causes. All are terrified about eating and/or digesting food, obsessed with food, and terrified of weight gain whatever their weight is. All have low self-esteem, damaging core beliefs, intelligence, and tend to be perfectionists. Some people fit the diagnostic criteria of two or more illnesses, and move between anorexic, bulimic and B.E.D. behaviour, having a totally *mixed eating disorder*.

Many people describe anorexia and bulimia as an illness spectrum: that is a continuum with anorexia at one end, and bulimia at the other, sufferers moving up and down this spectrum with time.

♠ **Figure 3: Questionable Anorexia-Bulimia Spectrum.**

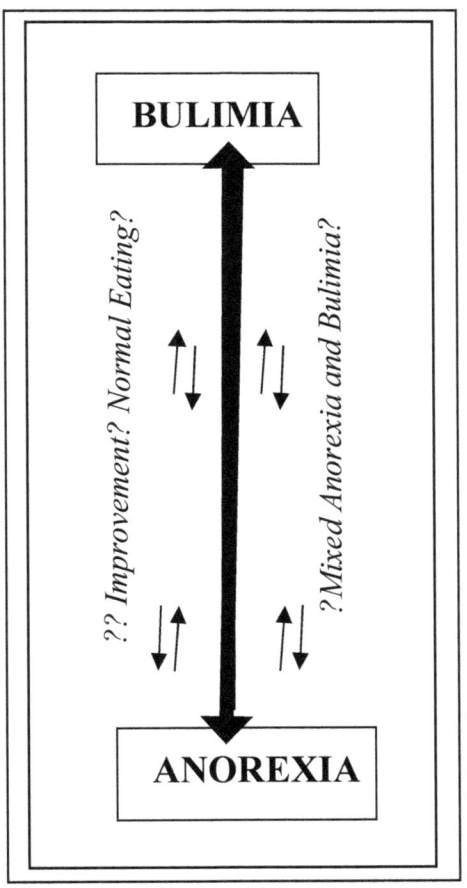

This is a useful tool to understand the illnesses' similarities and differences. But I ask, where is "normal" in this picture? And where is B.E.D? Instead of a continuum, I think of anorexia and bulimia as corners of a triangle. One corner is anorexia, one corner is bulimia, one corner is B.E.D, and E.D.N.O.S. forms a smaller triangle within the main one. Normality is somewhere in the middle. This helps people see how eating disorders of almost all kinds and normal eating are all interlinked, and can change over time; although any position on the chart below is just a "snapshot" in time. It also shows how polarised clinical eating disorders are compared to "normal." Three examples are given on the diagram next.

♠ **Figure 4: Normal, Borderline Disordered and Disordered Eating represented Diagrammatically.**

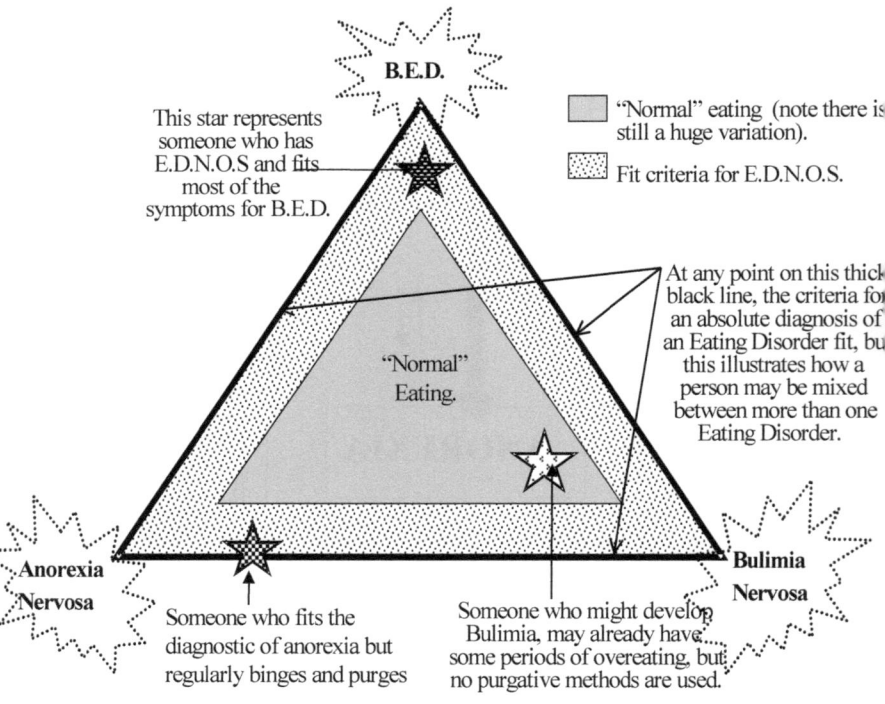

People can appear at any point on or in the larger triangle, wholly anorectic, wholly well, or somewhere mixed up right in between illnesses. Many sufferers move between illnesses over time. Many former anorectics become bulimic for example. This triangular representation seems to me, to portray a more realistic picture than simply thinking of anorexia and bulimia at two ends of an opposite spectrum.

Many people have days where their eating is strange. Someone with an eating disorder would regularly be at or near one of the edges of this diagram. Anyone within the spotted area (as labelled on the diagram) has disordered eating and would fit the criteria for E.D.N.O.S. but not *strictly* one particular eating disorder. Of course that person would be nearer to anorexia, bulimia, B.E.D., or a mixture; showing quite well how a person with E.D.N.O.S. is best treated for anorexia, or bulimia, B.E.D., or a mixture, depending on which diagnosis their problems fit most closely.

The inside triangle (the solid grey area) represents "normal" eating – whatever that means; showing how even within normality, people vary, and may be nearer to disordered eating of one type or another. Stars have been used to illustrate 3 possible positions people may find themselves at. Someone who is "mixed" or split 50:50 between anorexia and bulimia, fitting the criteria for both (although technically the diagnosis of anorexia would take precedence), would be half way along the thick bottom line. The thick black outside lines represent someone who fits the diagnostic criteria for an eating disorder; the corners represent a pure diagnosis of one specific diagnosis.

Movement from one to another eating disorders is always possible; indeed it is likely (within any

Reflective Reflections

timescale). Note that in terms of behaviour, a person may swing between anorexia, bulimia and B.E.D. within a year, month, week, day or matter of hours. A clinical diagnosis made by an expert would take a longer-term view of the eating disorder.

People (with and without eating problems) will change their position on this diagram over time – even within a day – for example, a person with bulimia may recover and eat normally whilst on holiday or in hospital, or may instead develop B.E.D. Movement from any point within the triangle to another is possible. Excluding some unusual eating disorders and illnesses (described later), everyone fits somewhere into this diagrammatic representation of eating. The combinations are endless...

I even imagine some people who I have known or who now, (as floating stars) lose touch with reality and drift off outside the triangle – those who die.

Chapter 6: Complex Needs.

> "Every man has his secret sorrows which the world knows not; and often times we call a man cold when he is only sad."
>
> ❧ Henry Wadsworth Longfellow (1807-1882)

Eating disorders are not only linked with depression and anxiety, they are linked with other psychiatric conditions, including manic depression (both bipolar I and bipolar II, and bipolar NOS), obsessive compulsive disorder (OCD), social phobia, post traumatic stress disorder (e.g. as a result of sexual abuse), personality disorders (e.g. borderline personality disorder), dissociative identity disorder (split personality - extremely rare), substance abuse, (deliberate) self-harm. There are even indications of a link between eating disorders and attention deficit disorder (ADD) and attention deficit and hyperactivity disorder (ADHD). Physical conditions including diabetes, M.E. and I.B.S. are also more common in people with eating disorders. Eating disorders combined with other disorders require special management and medications that can only be provided by professionals.

Do not despair if reading this you think you are a hopeless case, I was a mixture of _six_ of the above conditions, mainly severe mixed bipolar I affective disorder, *plus* anorexia and bulimia (hence an anorectic, sometimes non-purging type, sometimes purging type). I became ill when very, very young, and I beat it: so can you. I am now totally free of my anorexia, and have not substituted it for anything else.

It is worth making strikingly clear that people with eating disorders often have complex needs: most usually a combination of depression, and/or substance abuse problems. It is widely accepted that mood (affective) disorders are common in people with eating disorders, *all* eating disorders, although this not understood. To me it makes perfect sense, you feel bad so reduce what you eat to help you cope. For others they try to reduce weight healthily and they get sucked into the anorexia or bulimia. Anxiety surrounding many aspects of life is rampant. Suicidal ideation is also very common.[33] Co-morbid complications due to addiction to one or more substances are not rare.[34]

o **Mood Disorders in Eating Disorders.** [35]

Depression (of many types) is almost ubiquitous in eating disorder victims. Some propose that eating disorders cause depression and anxiety, and therefore recovery from the eating disorder should resolve the other psychological problems. But there is much evidence that depression and anxiety predate eating problems, and/or continue independently after recovery

---

[33] Cooper, PJ. (1995). *Eating Disorders and their relationship to Mood and Anxiety Disorders.* Brownell KD, & Fairburn CG, (Eds.) Eating Disorders and Obesity: A comprehensive handbook. New York: Guilford Press, p.159-164.

[34] Wilson, TG. (1995). *Eating Disorders Addictive Disorders.* Brownell KD, & Fairburn CG, (Eds.) Eating Disorders and Obesity: A comprehensive handbook. New York: Guilford Press, p.165

[35] Cynthia M. Bulik (2002) *Anxiety, Depression and Eating Disorders.* Eating Disorders and Obesity, A Comprehensive Handbook (Eds.) C.G. Fairburn and K.D. Brownell. Chapter 34 p. 193-198.

from disordered eating. My bipolarity has continued to be a massive part of my life even though I recovered from anorexia seven years ago. It was a part of my life for years before I became an anorectic. It is also suggested that eating disorders are sequelae (the result of) of depression and/or anxiety as opposed to vice versa. Eating disorders then most certainly worsen depression, manic depression, and/or anxiety worsens eating disorders. It works both ways and is individual to each person.

Some suggest that eating disorders, depression and anxiety are all symptoms of one
disease, but this is unlikely as so many people suffer from just one symptom alone. It is possible that one trigger (e.g. abuse) triggers depression in one person, and an eating disorder in another – depending on their personality, situation and genetic predisposition.

Another suggestion is a common biological factor, such as a neuroendocrine disturbance, which warrants further research. Finally the most likely suggestion is that eating disorders, mood disorders, and anxiety are separate illnesses, but they share some aetiological factors. Hence if you suffer from one, you have a greatly increased risk of suffering from another – as commonly occurs.

An example: An anorectic decides she wants to recover and gets help, she finds trying to recover extremely painful, upsetting and slow. Indeed she may very well get more ill before she starts to recover. This is likely to cause depression or worsen depression already present, especially in her malnourished state. A second example might be someone with depression who blames their low mood on times when they overeat – and ultimately develops bulimia as a "solution" to the depression – trust me, it works very well, for a while. The bulimic then begins to feel anxious about their vomiting technique, pushing them to vomit more and more each time. She/he starts keeping a bucket and bottles of water in their room in case someone else is using the bathroom, which might prevent purging. She/he feels anxious around people in case they have realised what he is doing, so she/he isolates her/himself, and starts to go running to ease the anxiety. Then he gets extremely anxious if he is prevented from running, and ends up going at four in the morning to make sure nobody can stop her/him... See how easily these problems can all interlink, and the possibilities are endless.

The two graphs below shows the results of a 2-month poll that took place in 2004 on the leading, international, sufferer-run website for eating disorders.[36] People were asked to report if they had or thought they had depression (of unspecified type – so including major depression and bipolar disorder) accompanying their eating disorder, and which eating disorder. This poll was intended to give an impression of concurrent depressive illness as perceived by sufferers. People were, as far as was possible to control on the Internet, allowed one vote only, and voted before seeing the results-so-far. I am not claiming this to be high quality research, but it is directly from sufferers, and it did receive 2,069 responses in a 2-month period. As you can see, other concurrent illnesses, especially depression, were exceedingly common in all eating disorders, as shown in figure five next.

---

[36] Something Fishy website. See recommended websites at the back of the book.

♠ **Figure 5: Prevalence of Depression (type unspecified) in people with Different Eating Disorders.**

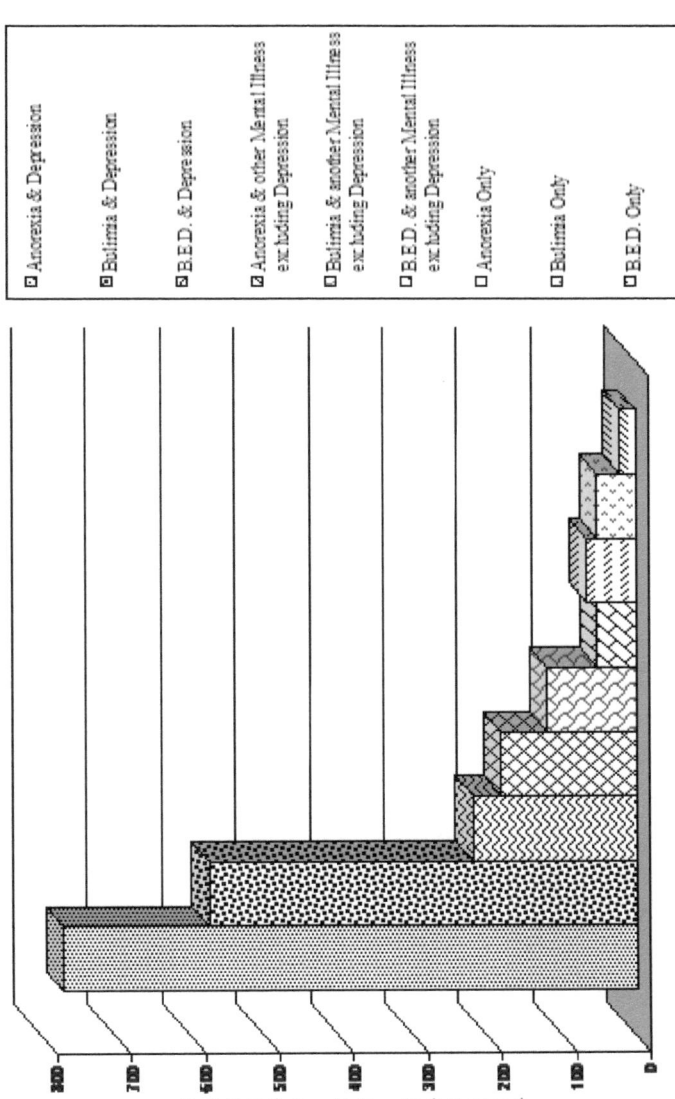

Reflective Reflections

Figure six next, from the same Internet poll, (n = 2,069) shows how many eating disorder sufferers feel their depression is recognised and being treated. It illustrates again how very common depression is in eating disorders with almost three quarters of eating sufferers reporting themselves as depressed. It is somewhat comforting to see that most people with depression did have a formal diagnosis, but still alarming to see that a significant proportion feel their depression is unrecognised.

♠ **Figure 6: Prevalence of Recognised and Unrecognised Depression (type unspecified) in people with Eating Disorders of all types.**

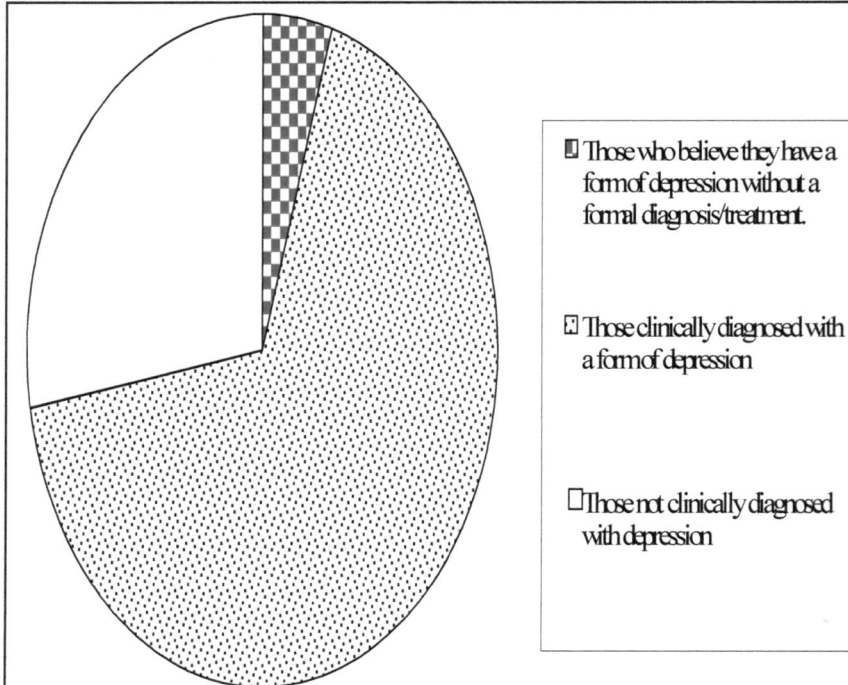

A recent 2004 article in the *International Journal of Eating Disorders* found that in two thirds of cases, depression *preceded* the eating disorder, which agrees with my personal experience and that of those sufferers I know. Anxiety preceding the eating disorder is also common. Both depression and anxiety that have an early onset are associated with a higher suicide risk. It is also suggested that people who have attempted suicide or feel suicidal are more likely to have developed depression before the eating disorder. Someone developing depression a year or more before subsequently developing an eating disorder is likely to present as someone who has attempted suicide or is suicidal. Those who are not suicidal are more likely to have developed depression as a result of the eating disorder. This postulates that those people who were depressed before the eating disorder have to suffer the initial depression/bipolar disorder, *plus* the awful depression that an eating disorder inevitably induces. (However, it is important not to get into competitions about who is suffering the most).

If a person is not depressed before the eating disorder develops, they most rapidly progress into depression due to malnutrition, desperation, self-hatred, anger, anxiety and so on. Self-harm, usually by cutting, is common. It is vital that anyone suffering from any form of mood disorder received proper treatment for their mood, for without concurrent treatment for depression/bipolar disorder, relapse, changing to another problem (e.g. anorexia to bulimia), worsening mood disorder, self-harm and suicidal ideation can result.

When using pharmacological treatments for eating disordered people with concurrent depression, the NICE guidelines suggest that caution should be used because the depressive symptoms may be alleviated by restoration of weight alone. I have *serious* misgivings about this recommendation. I believe mood disorders should always be treated with the utmost care and attention, aggressively, and irrespective of weight. Indeed, restoration of weight can be extremely difficult to cope with, and thereby worsen depression for a period.

o **Dependency issues.**

Addiction problems, past or present, in people with eating disorders, include street and prescription drugs, alcohol, laxatives, diet pills (herbal, over-the-counter and prescription). This is no reflection on eating disorder sufferers for being "weak," it is simply further illustration of the desperate and painful pathway their lives can take. For example, anorexia can cause insomnia due to both mood disorders and raised levels of the hormone adrenaline – hence a sufferer may turn to sleeping pills or alcohol to self-medicate. Since dependency problems are more common in people with eating disorders, is covariance seen in people seeking help for addiction problems? The answer is yes; this is precisely what has been shown to happen in groups of alcoholics. Alcoholics are more likely to have eating disorders than non-alcoholics.[37]

The use of diet pills, laxatives and diuretics (water pills) continues to be a problem despite serious health risks to various herbal and prescription medications. Examples include addiction to stimulant drugs such as amphetamine, cocaine, or the now banned "Fen-Phen,"

---

[37] Wilson, TG. (1995). *Eating Disorders Addictive Disorders.* Brownell KD, & Fairburn CG, (Eds.) Eating Disorders and Obesity: A comprehensive handbook. New York: Guilford Press, p.168

Fenfluramine and Dexfenfluramine prescription drug mixture, that causes cardiac valvular dysfunction (commonly leakage – which can be fatal). As mentioned, laxatives and diuretics cause weight loss in the form of water – and this can lead to life-threatening hypokalaemia (low blood potassium) – causing sudden death from heart attack. Despite the fact that most sufferers do realise weight loss is only water, "regaining" any weight, albeit water weight, can be hard or impossible to face, or seem like a quick fix to a bad day.

Eating disorders themselves are sometimes likened to addictions, and I think this is a true depiction. In order to be addictive there are three key factors the addictive 'whatever' must have/create: <u>tolerance</u>, <u>withdrawal</u> and <u>cravings.</u> This is very true of eating disorders, mainly psychological, but physically also. I believe that all eating disorders cause tolerance, the anorectic ever continuing to need to lose more weight to satisfy herself or she experiences withdrawal in the form of depression when not losing weight. The bulimic shows tolerance by bingeing and vomiting with increasing frequency and perhaps increasing size of binge. A binge eater may binge with greater frequency. For an anorectic stopping to lose weight or gaining weight causes a psychological craving to lose weight again. For the bulimic, when not bingeing there is definitely a physical (hunger) and psychological craving to return to disordered behaviour. When not bingeing a binge eater will crave a binge.

It is often argued that neither eating disorder has withdrawal symptoms, and as such cannot truly be addictions. But depends how you define withdrawal: I, and many sufferers would put forward a strong argument that cessation of eating disordered behaviour results in strong *psychological* withdrawal symptoms, such as severe depression, anxiety, confusion and/or stress. Some bulimics and binge eaters also suffer what could be considered as physical withdrawal symptoms from losing the sugar "high" they get from bingeing, and those anorectics who feel "high" from starving have to withdraw from feeling this "high."

All eating disorders are desperately hard to conquer and let go. I have dabbled in substances that are meant to be highly addictive. Not one of them comes close to the difficulty of giving up bulimia or anorexia. It was the hardest thing I did in my life. Other sufferers agree with this analogy.

o **Diabetes**

There is also a strong link between diabetes and eating disorders. People with insulin dependent diabetes mellitus (IDDM), also called "Type I diabetes" or "young-onset diabetes," are at increased risk of any eating disorder. It is entirely possible these people would develop eating disorders anyway, however the number of eating disordered people with IDDM is disproportionate, suggesting having diabetes is an additional risk factor. Unfortunately IDDM usually develops in people up to thirty, often much younger than thirty, and therefore appears at an age people are at the highest risk of independently developing an eating disorder. It is postulated that IDDM is linked to all eating disorders because people are forced to take an active interest in their diet in order to manage their diabetes.

Insulin dependent diabetes is a difficult illness to come to terms with, and people can feel depressed or rebel against their insulin regime and diet. As mentioned, *any* dieting, including focusing on a healthy diet, and watching sugar intake, is a risk factor for eating problems. Without giving too many dangerous details, I will just add that life-saving insulin can be abused to control weight, weight loss, and be purgative. Abuse of insulin can have serious health effects, short and long-term. Anyone with diabetes and an eating disorder will require specialised treatment.

o **Pregnancy.**

Women and girls with anorexia, bulimia and B.E.D. can get pregnant, although this is less likely in classical anorexia and where amenorrhea is a symptom. If you are pregnant and have an eating disorder then you *must* seek expert advice for the sake of your own health, and that of your unborn child. Note that physical health, and therefore a healthy diet, is important before pregnancy and when trying to get pregnant.

o **Myalgic Encephalopathy/ Encephalomyelitis (M.E.), also known as Chronic Fatigue Syndrome (C.F.S.)**

ME/CFS is a chronic, fluctuating illness. Its most common symptoms are severe fatigue, exhaustion, disordered sleep, gastric disturbances, and problems with memory, concentration and muscle pain. It is thought to affect up to 240,000 people in the UK.[38] There is some correlation (but not much literature) of M.E. and eating disorders. This might be because of loss of appetite due to M.E. causing weight loss that then gets out of control. It may also be caused due to the fact that eating healthily is important for M.E. sufferers, causing sufferers to focus on their diets. This focus can become problematic.

---

[38] Action for M.E. http://www.afme.org.uk/

○ Irritable Bowel Syndrome, (I.B.S.)

Irritable bowel syndrome affects a third of the population at some time in their life and about one in ten people suffer symptoms bad enough to drive them to see their doctor.[39] The most common symptoms of irritable bowel include: abdominal pain, spasms, diarrhoea, constipation, bloating, wind, and anxiety about general health and going out (for example if there is not a bathroom nearby).

There is some evidence (very little research has been done) linking I.B.S. with eating disorders. In these cases, cause and effect can be hard to establish. If someone with I.B.S. was to follow a diet, then they have been subjected to the leading cause of eating disorders, a diet, and thus, may develop one. It is also true that not eating properly, and in particular the use/abuse of laxatives can cause symptoms of I.B.S.

---

[39] The I.B.S. Network (UK based). http://www.ibsnetwork.org.uk/

Chapter 7: Eating Disorders: some tips from sufferers to carers and professionals.

Everyone should remember that weight has little to do with determining the good health or risk to the life of a person (including yourself) suffering with an eating disorder. Doctors, therapists, friends, family and anyone concerned with caring for a person should bear in mind the following fears that sufferers commonly describe.[40]

- *If I gain weight, they will think I am OK, but I'll actually feel much worse.*

- *I'm not thin enough.* (Even when emaciated).

- *They won't believe me.*

- *I'm not sick enough.*

- *They won't think I deserve help.*

- *They won't think I need help.*

- *No one takes me seriously.*

- *I'm too young or too old to be taken seriously.*

- *Even if they do help, the will abandon me when I still need them.*

- *They might force me into hospital.*

---

[40] With input from Something Fishy Eating Disorder Website: http://www.something-fishy.org/doctors/tips.php

Reflective Reflections

❖ *They might force me to eat.*

❖ *They might make me talk about painful issues.*

❖ *The doctor will tell my parents or people will find out.* (You are entitled to confidentiality, even under age if you are able to understand what is going on, in other words you are legally *compos mentis*. In the UK, once 16, you must be treated confidentially, (unless in the unlikely event you are to be detained under the Mental Health Act whereby your next of kin is informed of your detention, but they still only given minimal details).

❖ *The doctor/therapist/person I am asking for help will just see me as fat: they won't believe it's an eating disorder.* This could occur if someone underweight is and delusional, or if someone is overweight due to B.E.D.

❖ *The doctor is just going to make me gain/lose weight!* Professionals need to know that eating disorders are not about weight – weight change is a symptom.

❖ *My doctor/therapist will tell me to "just eat."*

❖ *My therapist refuses to treat me because I've lost/gained more weight.*

Punishment tactics do not work for eating disorders – they may appear to work short term, but they eat away at that person's self-esteem. **Coercion does not work**.

❖ *I'm a man and I know they'll think I'm weird, gay, or they won't believe me.*

❖ *How do I talk about my depression/drinking/drug use as well? I'm ashamed to talk about it.*

Chapter 8: Less well known and unofficial eating disorders, similar illnesses and behaviours.

❖ *Chewing and spitting* – food is tasted, chewed and then spat out. This is not a recognised eating disorder, but it does occur in people with anorexia, bulimia and E.D.N.O.S.

❖ *Prader-Willi syndrome* - A congenital condition whereby one symptom is a compulsion to eat constantly and not feel satiety. Sufferers are often institutionalised for life or they would literally eat themselves to death.

❖ *Anorexia Athletica* (compulsive exercising) as may take place as a compensatory measure to aid/maintain weight loss, (common in anorexia and bulimia) but this is not a formal diagnosis.

❖ *Body dysmorphic disorder* (BDD) is a formal psychiatric diagnosis, where sufferers obsess over one or more imagined physical defects in their appearance. BDD is not an eating disorder, although the sufferer may be obsessive about their weight or have a concurrent eating disorder and/or depression. BDD is a subtype of obsessive compulsive disorder (OCD).

❖ *Muscle dysmorphic disorder* ("bigorexia"), is not a formal diagnosis although it may be a form of BDD. People with this disorder obsess about being small and undeveloped and want to bulk up.

❖ *Infection-triggered, auto immune subtype of anorexia nervosa in young children* is not an official eating disorder, under research, possibly an autoimmune triggered illness.[41]

❖ *Orthorexia nervosa* is not an official eating disorder diagnosis, but common in anorexia and bulimia, as well as in otherwise healthy people. Named by Steven Bratman, M.D. to describe "a pathological fixation on eating 'proper' or 'pure' or 'superior' food."

❖ *Night-eating syndrome* - most food eaten late in the day or at night. Not a formal eating disorder.

❖ *Nocturnal sleep-related eating disorder* - Believed to be a sleep disorder, not an eating disorder. A person sleep eats and sleep walks – some people even sleep cook.

❖ *Rumination syndrome* – a person eats, swallows, and then voluntarily or involuntarily regurgitates food back into

---

[41] Journal of the American Academy of Child and Adolescent Psychiatry, Volume 36, Number 8.

Reflective Reflections

their mouth where it is chewed and swallowed again. Process may be repeated several times or for several hours per episode.

❖ *Gourmand syndrome* – preoccupation with fine (rich, expensive) food: acquisition, preparation, presentation, and consumption. This is exceedingly rare, and thought to be caused by injury to the brain.

❖ *Pica* – eating or craving non-food items such as dirt, clay, plaster, chalk, or paint chips.

Chapter 9: Eating Disorders and the Dangers of the Internet.

"You can never be too thin…"

&. Websites promoting eating disorders.

There are many wonderful, helpful websites created to inform, support and encourage the recovery of those affected by all eating disorders and co-disorders (like SomethingFishy, details at the back of the book). Unfortunately, around 1998 pro eating disorder sites began springing up, hitting the news in 2001. These sites are designed to encourage anorexic and/or bulimic behaviour, by encouraging eating disorders as "lifestyle choices" rather than psychiatric illnesses. They share dangerous tips on how to become a "better" anorectic or bulimic, and support or compete with each other to lose weight. It is strongly recommended that you do *not* seek these sites out. I know some of you will…

Pro anorexia websites, or "Pro-Ana" sites as they are called, are laced with pictures of bony women, ranging from skinny celebrities to at-death's-door emaciation. These pictures *trigger* negative emotions in anorexic people, making them feel inadequate, and cause them want to lose weight. Pictures of women starving and looking days from death are portrayed as beautiful and desirable – the intent is to motivate others to also lose weight to such extremes, so called "Thinspiration." Some people look at these pictures to intentionally aid their own weight loss, but others are essentially tricked in to looking at these pictures, and suffer more as a consequence. Pro-bulimia website, or "Pro-Mia" sites allow people to discuss bingeing, purging, and

Reflective Reflections

technique tips – which are often very dangerous. Discussion of food and eating, compounded by web pages covered with pictures of "naughty/bad" fattening food has the very real risk of triggering bingeing. Often Pro-Ana sites target both anorexia and bulimia victims.

Can you imagine the backlash if someone set up a pro diabetes, pro cancer or pro depression website – people would be angry at these serious physical and mental disorders not being treated properly. Anorexia, bulimia and B.E.D are serious mental and physical illnesses.

I do not think that the people who set up these websites are intentionally malicious: rather they are misguided and ill. *These websites are dangerous*, but I believe very strongly in freedom of expression and therefore I would not ban them. I would educate strongly against them. Many things in life are dangerous. Some people do derive support from these sites that helps them to survive; some sites have warnings with their Pro-Ana advice. I do think people need serious warnings to avoid such sites altogether, especially if they have a history of an eating disorder or other mental health problems. Better warnings are needed to caution people as/if they choose to enter these websites. Parents should know what their children look at on the Internet – it is not a safe place. I'm sure some of you will put this book down right now, and look up these sites – but at least you are forewarned. I hope most of you wont. (There are no such sites recommended at the end of this book).

The Pro-Ana movement exists; there is even a philosophy for pro-anorexia. "Pro-Ana" is said to be short for proactive, volitional[42] anorexia. It is very dangerous, absolute rubbish, but plenty of very ill

---

[42] A deliberate, intentional act or choice.

people out there disagree with me. I never doubted I was ill, perhaps that makes me lucky; or perhaps these kids are just wannabe-anorectics who create some ill people and drag down all the really ill people who find their websites when looking for tips and encouragement.

The dangerous Pro-Ana "Philosophy."

> *"There are No Victims Here. Pro-anorexia is not a disease or a disorder. It is not to be confused with eating-disordered-anorexia. It is not something invasive that one "suffers from." It is a lifestyle choice that begins and ends with a particular faculty human beings seem in drastically short supply of today: the will."*

Most Pro-Ana websites (note that most Pro-Ana are aimed at people with anorexia and/or bulimia) have "The Thin Commandments," "The Ana Creed," and the "The Ana Prayer." I imagine they are rather brainwashing to young minds and I am hugely grateful that they were not in existence when I was a teenager. I feel these websites cheapen eating disorders; they make a serious mental illness seem like a stupid, superficial and normal teenage behaviour. Eating disorders are not about looking pretty or being a trendy website "Ana-faerie;" (as members call each other). They kill, maim and destroy.

The (NONSENSE) Thin Commandments:

1. If you aren't thin you aren't attractive.
2. Being thin is more important than being healthy.

Reflective Reflections

3. You must buy clothes, cut your hair, take laxatives, starve yourself, and do anything you can to make yourself look thinner or be thinner.
4. Thou shall not eat without feeling guilty.
5. Thou shall not eat fattening food without punishing oneself afterwards.
6. Thou shall count calories and restrict intake accordingly.
7. What the scale says is the most important thing.
8. Losing weight is good; gaining weight is bad.
9. You can never be too thin.
10. Being thin and not eating are signs of true willpower and success.

How about this direct quote from a Pro-Ana website:

"People can live without food indefinitely as long as they have water."

Erm, no, I think not. It is a rather well established FACT that people die without food. Usually the thinner a person is to begin with the more quickly they will die from lack of food.

Below are some comments taken from "Ana's Creed," (in italics) sayings appearing on many Pro-Ana websites, followed by my counter comments:

"I believe in Control, the only force mighty enough to bring order to the chaos that is my world."

Anorexia controls the victim, not vice versa. Control is all an illusion, a convincing and deadly delusion. The thinner you get, the longer you are ill, the more the feeling of control feels true, but the truth is that the person is *more* out of control.

> *"I believe that I am the most vile, worthless and useless person ever to have existed on this planet, and that I am totally unworthy of anyone's time and attention. I believe that people who tell me differently must be idiots. If they could see how I really am, then they would hate me almost as much as I do."*

How very sad – and quite revealing that on websites claiming that anorexia is a "lifestyle choice," such self-hatred is apparent and standard. It actually demonstrates the presence of a mental disorder. How can you call something a "lifestyle choice" when it means you must detest yourself this much. I remember feeling the same way even though it was/is not true. This made it almost impossible to help me – but not totally impossible.

> *"I believe in calorie counters as the inspired word of god, and memorise them accordingly."*

Well that's just f**king nuts.

> *"I believe in bathroom scales as an indicator of my daily successes and failures."*

Our value is not measured by weight, but by what we do and who we are.

> *"I believe in a wholly black and white world, the losing of weight, recrimination for sins,*

Reflective Reflections

the abnegation[43] of the body and a life ever fasting."

Of course, a life like that results in two things: misery and death. A black and white world is cruel; it just looks easy from the outside. Self-punishment is always pointless. Losing weight and a "life ever fasting" are not sustainable, and will *kill* you or someone you care for.

One girl's reply to a Pro-Ana website was revealing:

"Dear Ana,

I feel trapped by you.

Where is the love you promised? The acceptance?

When will I feel like I'm finally in control?

Why is it that the more I control what I eat and weigh, the more out of control I feel? As I peel away the layers of fat, the old problems resurface ... the depression, the loneliness, the cutting, the insomnia, the self-hate."

Here is a shortened example of a section taken from the Pro-Ana and Pro-Mia 'Bible' on a Pro-Ana website in 2010.

---

[43] Self-denial and/or the setting aside of personal needs to follow a belief.

Ana, Mia and me

Ana is my angel and my devil. She's my friend and my foe.
Sometimes I want her to stay forever and sometimes I just want her to go
She comforts me when I'm down, comfort through distraction
through hunger pains, and cramps, cravings and body reactions.
She's always here with me, she tells me what to do
when to eat and sleep and exercise and what size should be my goal.

She is there when I hurt and when I feel the pain
When I lose some inches or shed a few pounds,
I can feel her approval, like she's smiling down.
But when I gain some weight or cave in to a craving
The wrath of ana befalls upon me with a whirlwind of guilt and self-hating.

I'm tired of hiding her from the world, I'm tired of the secrets, lies, and deceiving.
Is it wrong to want people to accept who I am, my ana is part of me.
So why do they say I'm sick?
Why do they frown and shake a fist?
There's nothing wrong with me! It's a lifestyle, can't you see?
I want to see my beautiful bones and feel as light as rain.
I want to be thin more than anything, after all, beauty takes pain!

"What game shall we play today?"
I don't feel like playing, I'd like to rest if I may.
"No, we will play a game. Chocolate cake, apple pie…"

Reflective Reflections

I'm not hungry, Mia, please hear my cry.
...And so it came to be that Mia had won,
Delivering her Ana to a weight of a ton.
Chocolate cake and apple pie Mia demanded,
If ana said no, she would've surely been reprimanded.

So it went that Ana gobbled the food,
All the while Mia continued her attitude.
Ana cried and cried with a force so strong,
Until Mia finally sang her song.
"Ugly, stupid, lazy, and fat,"
Mia ordered the helpless little girl to her knees,
Begging for forgiveness, Mia would not hear her pleas.

Three strong sons of evil pushed down back,
Ana struggled and wept, finally feeling her courage crack.
Chocolate cake and apple pie filled the bowl,
Mia's strength had taken its toll.
Repeated and repeated until Ana could take no more,
Mia laughed and said, "Good girl, you've done my chore."

These sites still exist: they are being deleted but they just reappear elsewhere. Therefore as a warning to all, I include a real, (edited for safety) example of a website conversation about anorexia. Details about how to hide anorexia, tips on eating less, purging, misusing substances including drugs and discussion of actual weight figures have been removed, and even then you will see there is an interesting debate illustrating clear delusional thinking in those who are ill. What you read may seem unbelievable but it is totally genuine. "Rexie" is short for anorexia. In this discussion Antagonist 2 was actually I – Katy Sara Culling – whilst still anorexic but recovering well.

April: I'm tired of all the crap about anorexia being a disorder, it is a way of life which people should embrace and understand.

Liz: Are you under X lbs yet??

April: It makes me so sad that people cannot just learn that anorexia is like a philosophy. Yes, I got under X lbs yesterday!! I'm so excited.

Liz: Congrats on getting under X lbs, it starts getting easier now.

Antagonist 1: Weirdo's.

Liz: It is a way of life.

Antagonist 2: You won't have a life if you keep starving yourselves.

Liz: Once I was having a really good week and I cracked and ate a sandwich. Don't you hate that feeling? You're doing so well and than you break, and you can actually *see* all the weight you gained.

Antagonist 1: If starving yourself to death isn't proof of something wrong then nothing is.

Liz: I am a proud rexie and my body is beautiful. Would you rather I be fat? This way I don't have ridiculous love handles which pour over the edges of my tight fitting clothing. This way I have a tiny figure

Reflective Reflections

with sexy ribs and bones popping out. What I do is right and there is no stopping me.

April: Liz you totally get it! How many ribs you got showing??? I have 2 normally and 3 if I bend a little.

Liz: I have two ribs showing, on my good days three.

Antagonist 2: I'd rather you live. Do you know that it isn't only a choice between being a skeleton and being fat? There's a whole shade of normal in between. Do you know why you feel the need to be *so* thin *so* much?

Antagonist 1: There is a HUGE gap between fat and a walking skeleton. You are ill.

April: I HAVE NO MENTAL DISORDER! My doctor says it is perfectly normal to want to be thin and no treatment is necessary.

Antagonist 2: Don't you like hearing the truth? And what the hell sort of doctor are you going to? Or did you hide your body? You implied you have and want anorexia, everything you've said in here suggests that you do. Your own words are that you want to choose anorexia. Yet it is well recognised and classified as a mental disorder.

April: Anorexia is not a mental disorder, we are not sick; we make our choices for a reason.

Liz: Just because some doctor scientist people decided anorexia is bad, doesn't make it so. People are so set in their stupid beliefs its disgusting.

Antagonist 2: !?!?!?!?!? Is this a wind up?

April: Today I ate half a carrot in one sitting, I felt so fat!!

Liz: April don't worry, half a carrot is fine, just don't eat anything else.

Antagonist 1: It is clear the anorexia you suffer from is also eating away at your brain cells.

Liz: If I start dying I'll eat more, it's really not anymore complicated than that, so why are you people trying to make it?

Antagonist 2: You do know that it's *not* that simple don't you? You don't "just" start to eat more when you decide to. You are building a perilous relationship between feeling good and not eating. You are not in control. You think you are, but you are not. Look up the word DENIAL. In Psychiatry it means "a defence mechanism that blocks out painful thoughts." In your case it means not admitting, even to yourself, that you have a serious illness, and, not coping with all the reasons that lead you to choose this

Reflective Reflections

dangerous pathway. You are not facing up to needing help.

Antagonist 1: OK Let's try and have a real debate. Your body is a biological system in equilibrium. If it doesn't get food then it starts eating into itself.

Liz: Yeah that's the whole point! I want my body to eat itself, then I get smaller.

Antagonist 2: You have a serious problem. I recognise it because I've been there too. But you are doing damage to your body and will die if this goes on. You cannot maintain this way of life and live productively, happily, and healthily. Yes you will get smaller as your body uses your organs, like your heart, to digest and provide energy for life. *You're not digesting fat; you're digesting life.*

Liz: I hate eating. Nothing makes me feel more disgusting and ugly.

Antagonist 2: I'm sorry to hear that. It is classically anorectic. You can get help, and change.

Liz: Doctors etc. They really don't get it they aren't right about everything, anorexia is fine if you know what your doing.

Antagonist 2: Do you really know what you are doing? I know you *think* you do, but one day you will realise the truth. Anorexia tricks you into thinking you control it. But it traps you; controls you, and if you let it, it will control you to death. Look what it does to you – you're freezing cold all the time and have no energy. Has your hair started to fall out yet? Your skin gets all yellow and wrinkly. Your body starts burning your muscles and the organs for energy – do you want your heart to be eaten away at? Pro-Ana is a death sentence.

I am certain there will be Pro-Ana's reading this book, furious at my damnation of their beliefs. The illnesses, Ana and Mia are treated almost like beloved but demanding and relentless old *friends*. I am equally certain that *every single one of them* will one day look back upon their time as a Pro-Ana and know that they were in fact, very ill indeed. That is except for those that will die of course...

Chapter 10: Personal experience stories from people with eating disorders

> "He who has not looked on Sorrow will never see Joy."
>
> ❧ Kahlil Gibran (1883-1931)

o **Non-survivor personal experience of anorexia.**

Karen Carpenter died at the age of just 32 on February 4, 1983. She died of a cardiac arrest despite the fact she was on the road to recovery at the time; showing how dangerous anorexia nervosa is to physical health. She was 5'4", but weighed only 108lbs (7½ stone, 49kgs). Her death, whilst a tragedy, brought anorexia and eating disorders out of their secretive closets, exploded into the media, and more importantly into the medical (psychiatric and psychological) professions, and research. Heed Karen's warning: *don't miss it all* which she said she feared she might do.

o **Survivor (so far) personal experience of anorexia by Lynne Moore.**

The first thing I always seem to say to people when they ask about my eating disorder, is that I never chose it, I didn't intentionally wake up one morning and think oh I wont eat today, which is what many people who I met think, from family to friends, and perhaps that's what my understanding would have been more like if I'd never had to go through it myself. It's portrayed so much in the public eye as though it's just a simple choice. If only it was that easy.

I guess it kind of crept up on me, I didn't realise I had an eating disorder, then I denied having an eating disorder and by then the eating disorder had taken control of me. I guess at 24 the idea of developing an eating disorder made me deny it even more and it wasn't as though I stood in front of the mirror thinking I was fat. I now know there's so much more to an eating disorder

It started so gradually but then took a quick grip, just missing the odd meal, cutting out what I considered 'bad foods,' being continually on the go from the moment of waking and squeezing in exercise routines.

For me it was very much to do with control, many things had happened in my life up to that point that I had no control of, and was having severe panic attacks and anxiety. By controlling what I put inside me I had the power back, each time the number on the scales went down I felt a sense of achievement from controlling myself so well. But then if the scales didn't move or had gone up, that made me miserable and even more strict with myself - it meant I was a failure, greedy and I didn't deserve whatever extra I'd eaten to increase the number.

I restricted my food even more and more, perhaps eating a spoonful of vegetables a day with the odd jelly sweet, I restricted all my fluids, weighed myself every day usually more than once, if I had a day where I'd eaten a little extra I would try to make myself sick. I kept a food diary just to see how little I could eat each day. I became sneaky, nasty and lied – all traits I can't stand in others. I wanted to push everyone away and stay in my little bubble where I could do what I wanted. Reading books on eating disorders for hints and tips or on the Internet. I didn't trust people just wanted to help me; everyone had an ulterior motive of just forcing food down me.

My diary at this point consisted every day of a note of my weight, what I'd managed to miss out in food or do to cancel it out. Looking back the only words I really used were all to do with weight, control and many names I would call myself. A sentence that featured a lot was the only time I feel good is when I don't eat anymore.'

It wasn't until the first time I went to see a dietician that the word anorexia nervosa was used in relation to me, I remember being stunned, and they must have been talking about somebody else. Up until then the GP and anyone else I met had referred to an eating disorder. I absolutely hated the word anorexia and refused to say it and accept that was what was wrong with me - I was not one of the people you see on TV or in magazines.

The biggest shock came when I was asked to go into hospital voluntarily, and if I didn't agree it wouldn't be long until I'd be taken in anyway. I had come to the point where I felt like I was begging someone to help me, I was so tired, and wanted to sleep until it had all gone away. I remember meeting a doctor at the time who said to me if I didn't eat at home what made me think they could help me eat in hospital. I fell apart then and believed there was no hope.

I can remember the whole time in hospital like it was yesterday, from the noises, smells, people, food etc. I was on an adult's mental health ward as there was no specialist eating disorder unit near by. There were many people with different mental health problems and to be honest without them I wouldn't of stayed as long as I did. Not having to deal with many patients with an eating disorder I suppose gave me more opportunity to carry on as I had been, I could exercise and wouldn't remind staff if it was a snack time.

There were some lovely staff, but some that treated me like a child, asking if I was just doing it for attention, or telling me off in front of the other patients for not scraping my yoghurt pot clean. My aim was to eat and get out of there so I could go back to how I was before going in, that life was better than being stuck in there. The only issue that everyone was dealing with was my low weight and not all the reasons that had got me to that point. After 6 weeks I discharged myself, looking back now I probably did leave acting like a child the psychiatrist from the hospital said to me, "I know you wont leave," something inside me snapped and I rung home saying I was leaving and within a few hours was packed and home.

I knew my family would come for me; they'd hated me being in there and just wanted to protect me. I owe them so much, I did nothing but push them away and yet they never left my side. I've really found out who my true friends and family are and can't thank them enough for putting up with me and sticking with me.

Now I knew how much I could eat and exercise and keep at a certain weight so things just gradually reverted back to how they'd been before.

By the Christmas I'd begun self-harming and just wanted my life over. I'd had enough and was planning what I needed to do. The crisis team were then called in. I don't believe I actually wanted to die, but was so fed up, and couldn't see this ever changing the thought of living

Reflective Reflections

everyday fighting something in my mind to eat I didn't want to do. I saw them for just over a month and managed to convince them all I was over it.

I suppose the part of me that wouldn't trust anyone else left me feeling all alone, which in some ways I wanted but others I just wanted someone to give me a hug and say we can fix this - I wouldn't of believed them if they had.

I gave up so many times that year, feeling worthless, disgusting, with no way out. My head constantly thinking of food, how and when to exercise, purging, panic attacks, hating leaving the house and being in crowded places, crying or wanting to cry but not letting myself. Shutting myself off from all my friends, I'd had to resign from my job, starting to take pills to numb the pain, more than what I was prescribed, and to me the worst of all was cutting myself. (I've seen people's reactions to this, which makes me feel ashamed of it). At this same point my sessions with my psychologist ended not in the best way. The one person I had really believed I could trust had deserted me. It all came to a head, on a day that made me see how capable of hurting myself I could be.

However I'm still here. From looking back I can see the changes I have made, like controlling my panic and anxiety, getting out and about again, beginning college part time, the understanding I have of my ED and many of the reasons that got me here. But everyday I'm still fighting, fighting that gremlin in my head, I still have big problems with food and obsessive exercise and still self-harm and to be honest cannot picture a time when things will be even slightly better. Just to get to a point of going to work again.

I worry so much over other people's judgements and

reactions to the eating disorder and me. When I meet new people I desperately want to say I'm just me not me with what feels like – a big flashing anorexic sign above my head.

But then the biggest critic of myself is me, I can call myself enough things and can hate myself more than anyone else ever possibly could. I really do believe the only reason I am still here is because of my GP, who despite everything I've told him and everything I've done, has been there continuously with support and humour, making someone smile really can lift their day.

I've been seeing a nutritionist to who works voluntarily through Beat – who used to be called The Eating Disorder Association - Many of the things I'm working through now is at more of a pace that when I make a change I'm more likely to stick with it. I no longer ask myself "Why has this happened to me?" instead I say "Why not me?"

o **Survivor personal experience of bulimia by Katy Sara Culling.**

Technically I was an anorectic bulimic, but for several years of my life bulimia dominated my life. I can still remember the first time I made myself sick. I was about 13, in my bedroom, and had eaten a bag of jellied sweets. I went to the bathroom, leaned over the sink and stuck two fingers down my throat. I didn't know if it would work, but it did, and I went away content that I hadn't just eaten all that candy. I can't remember the 2nd, 3rd or 10th time I made myself sick. I know that for a month or more I just used to throw up my evening meal, as quietly and quickly as possible. I was overweight and losing weight fast. This went on for some time.

Reflective Reflections

I remember that at some point, again I cannot pinpoint exactly when, I decided that if I were going to throw up my dinner I may as well eat some more food before I was sick. So I got into the habit of eating dinner, then going upstairs and eating some crisps and chocolate, then making myself sick. Because I'd eaten such bad foods I forced myself to drink a pint of water to washout my stomach and be sick again. I loved food, it was like there was a part of my brain that lit up when I was eating, and that was sad and grey when I wasn't.

I learned to eat soft sloppy foods because they were always easiest to throw up and I always finished my binges with ice cream which was the easiest food to get the process of being sick started. I sometimes had to virtually shove my whole hand into my mouth to get enough of a gag reflex to start the vomiting. Once it got going it was easier.

I used to get a pan, melt butter in it, I love anything with butter in it, then I would add double cream and grated cheese to make a cheese sauce, and I'd always have a huge plate of that with pasta, usually ravioli. The stuff didn't even taste too bad coming back up, it wasn't down there long enough to mix with my stomach acid and therefore taste like normal vomit. In other words, the vomiting wasn't that unpleasant.

I would make myself wash out my stomach with water and keep on being sick until all that came back was water. I also started each binge with a tomato sandwich to line my stomach, I didn't mind if I digested some of it, and seeing some tomato coming back up was always a relief, it meant, so I thought, that I had got rid of the fatty food I'd eaten after – I assumed the food came back up in the reverse order to how I'd eaten it... ice cream first, pasta, then sandwich for example, though I usually ate more than that. Thousands of kcals or kJ, whichever term for energy you use.

My underweight weight levelled out whilst I did this – I wanted to lose weight, but the power the food had over me and the relief of any binge had such a power over me that whilst I swore each time was the last, sometimes I'd finish vomiting and go straight into another binge. Looking back I don't know why I ever binged. The first two or three mouthfuls were heavenly but after that I don't think I tasted any of it.

Of course it had the advantage of using up time, and that was a massive help to me because I suffer from bipolar disorder and was depressed. When depressed time drags – any binge/vomit session would take up at least 3 hours where I would be numb from the pain because I was focussed on the food totally, whichever direction it was heading. It was a great distraction to my mood, made me exhausted so I slept better and of course I felt like I had jumped through time.

When I was manic I would do stupid things like buy smoked salmon and delicacies from expensive shops like gorgeous Marks & Spencer foods and binge on them. I still tried to vomit it all up but was less bothered by it when manic because I felt better about myself and the food I'd eaten was all gourmet shit. I'd usually gain a few pounds when manic. I paid for all this on a credit card that my father paid off each month so I could have anything I wanted. Even when he realised what I was doing he didn't take the card away from me, I think he realised I really, truly *needed* it.

Things really got out of hand when I went to university. I didn't make any real friends because they all saw I was very thin and had no patience for the anorectic-bulimic girl... and anyway I would usually stay in during the evenings to binge and vomit (I had an en-suite room) so I was very lonely. Then I stopped going to lectures because it meant I could start my binge vomit cycle earlier – somehow I was relieved when it was over, then I could relax for the rest of the day. I typically binged three times followed each time by three vomiting sessions – and I really washed out my stomach as I was managing to retain an underweight weight and this pleased me. My BMI dropped fast as I ate nothing other than what was in binges. I did drink vodka though, neat. It was the only way to get to sleep. By the end of the first year I found myself drinking daily, bingeing daily, vomiting daily, and being called to do re-sits in my exams during the summer.

Instead I explained that I had an eating disorder and had missed most lectures and asked to repeat the year in a new department, this was granted. I repeated the year in a new department but fitted my bingeing, vomiting and drinking around lectures this time. I even made a few friends on my course, but no friends where I lived because I needed to have my privacy to binge. I had often wondered if any of my floor-mates realised what I was doing. Could my neighbour hear me vomiting? The walls were thin. If they knew or suspected, none of them said a single word to me about my bulimia to me. That suited me fine at the time.

At the end of my second year I finally got into a treatment program near my home – this meant I had to ask for another year off, though I planned to return. The program was a day hospital where they fed you lunch and tea. You arrived at 10a.m. You were supposed to eat breakfast yourself at home – I never did of course. Lunch was at 12p.m. on the dot, a starter, main meal, and pudding. We were given 30 minutes to eat it. Then we were observed for 45 minutes to make sure we didn't vomit. To be honest I could still have got some up after the 45 minutes but I wanted to get better, so I didn't make myself sick.

What was difficult was having to eat another meal at 4pm when not at all hungry, but the staff wanted to go home at 5pm so you just had to accept it. Most people with eating disorders like to leave the food they are going to eat until late in the day as it is small and precious, and so it is something to be looked forward to. If I had my own way I would eat then go to sleep. The program was uncomfortable and it would have been very easy to be sick but by then I had found a dogged determination that I was not going to let this beat me. I used to go swimming every evening to make me feel I'd worked off some of the food eaten. Usually once I got out of the pool I no longer felt uncomfortable enough to want to make myself sick, and as I was satiated I didn't feel like bingeing. I still drank a good glass of vodka to help me sleep.

One day one of the nurses noticed the self-harm marks on my arm. That week, at the age of 21 I had my first psychiatrist appointment. He diagnosed me as having depression and prescribed a different antidepressant. (I had been on 60mg of Prozac to treat the bulimia) I was fine with taking a new antidepressant but it said not to drink alcohol with it. I stopped drinking. This meant I didn't sleep much, so I used the time to exercise. I actually started to lose weight so on weighing day I had a bag of two penny pieces in my pocket and that made it look like I'd stayed the same weight. They added a snack to my regimen at 2p.m. So much food crammed into such a small period of time. I had to add another bag of coins the following week and I'd still lost weight. I endured lectures about exercise.

It was all very intimidating, 3 members of staff would watch us at the table – they'd tell people off for eating disorder behaviours. For example, one girl to my right used to mash all her food together until she just had a messy blob on her plate – then giving her credit – she ate it all. She would get told off for that mashing though. I would get told off for eating too slowly. A friend of mine got told off for putting too much pepper on her food. (She told me that she did it to make the food taste disgusting, as she didn't deserve to eat nice food). I found it very hard to be criticised and watched in the manner they did it. I stuck with it though and got up to my target weight (with two rolls of coins and a stone in my pockets). We weren't allowed to talk about food during or after the meal.

I wont lie and say I never binged or threw up again, but over the following year whilst I was at home waiting to get back to university I just found my brain focussing more on the unpleasant purging and less on the pleasant binge, which lead me to give it up for good. I must add that I had a lot of help from my GP who saw me often.

It's now been over a decade since I binged or vomited on purpose. The idea of either is completely alien to me. Giving it up was hell and I'm never going back there again.

o **Survivor personal experience of B.E.D. by Sarah Mercer.**

I've been anorexic (restrictive type and purging type) and bulimic but both of these eating disorders were my way of responding to the terror of what felt to me the most 'shameful' eating disorder and my 'default', B.E.D. I can't even say the words, at best I use the acronym.

I suppose for me all three eating disorders share more similarities than differences, absolute fear of food and core beliefs about greed and guilt about eating or desiring food that lead to my use of eating disordered behaviours. As a teen I was slim, active and ate well. I had a balanced diet yet still enjoyed meals out, take-aways and junk food in moderation. I couldn't see that, I only recognised that I enjoyed food and felt guilty for that.

Over time the guilt and shame grew and this seemed to fuel my use of food as some sort of convoluted mechanism to provide both comfort and punishment. It would start by desiring some nice 'treats' to make myself feel better about the emptiness and loneliness I felt in my late teens but as soon as I ate I'd feel so guilty, not so much for eating but for enjoying eating. Then the urge to eat more and more hit, until the comfort element was lost and the punishment dominated.

Over time my binges got bigger, as did my terror and shame. My weight was spiralling and although I never became overweight I did end up much higher than my body's set point in a very short period of time. I could imagine my parents looking in and wondering how I could be so out of control and weak to let this happen to myself. Every day I'd get up, determined for things to be different. Some days I tried (unsuccessfully) to restrict my food intake, other days I'd try a more balanced meal plan. All ended up in the same result. I needed the oblivion of an evening of bingeing to block out painful feelings of sadness and shame. All the while I was fuelling these feelings by acting in this way.

Each day the urge to overeat would be there, I'd fight it for a while until it just felt easier to give in. The moment

Reflective Reflections

I'd snap there would be relief, I'd enjoy the first few things I ate. At the same time the panicked thoughts of 'I'm out of control, I can't believe I've done it again, I'm going to end up morbidly obese' took over. I'd feel hopeless and despondent and keep eating until I felt so full I couldn't fit any more in. I'd then lie on my bed, writhing in agony – praying for my body to give up, for my stomach to rupture and it all be over, I'd sweat from the sheer volume of carbohydrate and sugar rich food in my body. Eventually I'd sleep a little, having nightmares and sweats. Then a new day would dawn and I'd have to get up and figure out how to approach food again that day when still feeling over-full from the night before but knowing that if I missed meals I'd set up another binge.

It was chaos, and absolute hell. I had no routine, I tried so many approaches, meal plans, flexible eating, trying to respond to my hunger, trying not to deprive myself. Nothing worked, the only certainty I had was that each day I would get up and have to figure out what clothes would still fit my expanding body, pretty soon there were none, and soon after that the new larger ones were too tight, and so on...

The chaos of the binge cycle drove me into a very dark place of suicidal ideation and severe self harm. Each day I'd think, 'I can't do this, I can't face food, I just want someone to take it out of my hands'. However my guilt about my overeating made it impossible to let people help. I did manage to tell my GP and psychiatrist but their response seemed to confirm to me that I didn't have a 'real' problem, I was a 'normal' weight (my BMI was normal, however it had jumped from 18 to 24 in about 8 weeks, which was dismissed). I'd like the professionals to realise just how much despair B.E.D. can bring and how serious it is. I would never have developed anorexia and bulimia if I'd have been able to get help with B.E.D. The only way I found to get rid of it was to swap to another eating disorder.

As for the severity of the condition, I have never been more suicidal, reckless, desperate, trapped and out of control than when consumed by B.E.D. compared even to a time when anorexic (binge-purge type) with a BMI of 15.

Chapter 11: HOPE.

> "Man can live about forty days without food,
> about three days without water,
> about six minutes without air,
> but only for one second without hope."
>
> ❧ Anonymous

I NEVER thought I would overcome my eating disorder. It had run on for far too long and was deeply ingrained in my existence: 15 years ruined, and nothing seemed to work. I was a textbook *chronic* anorectic. I know the same hopelessness was/is true of many good friends of mine. One has since died from starvation alone; the rest of us soldier on, either recovered or recovered enough. I guess we all cling to some little piece of hope, however small, and for most of us, it has paid off.

I am totally free of anorexia, I still get anorectic thoughts but I know how to totally ignore them! You can recover too. I was once totally trapped. What's the old saying? "If I can do it you can do it too." Let that give you hope.

Useful Websites and books.

My website: http://www.katysaraculling.com/

Alcoholics Anonymous (Global).
Website: http://www.aa.org/

American Psychiatric Association
Website: www.psych.org/

American Psychological Association
Website: www.apa.org/

Strongly recommended
Beat
Website: http://www.b-eat.co.uk/Home

Mind (National Association for Mental Health) UK based
0845 7660163
Website: http://www.mind.org.uk/

National Alliance for the Mentally Ill
Website: www.nami.org/

The Samaritans
Website: www.samaritans.org/

SANE (UK)
Website: http://www.sane.org.uk/

STRONGLY RECOMMENDED:
The Something Fishy pro recovery website for all eating disorders
Website: http://www.something-fishy.org/

NICE: National Institute of Clinical Excellence, National Health Service, (UK).

Reflective Reflections

Website: http://www.nice.org.uk/

Narcotics Anonymous (Global).
Website: http://www.na.org/

National Institute of Mental Health (USA)
Website: http://www.nimh.nih.gov/

Recommended Books:

Dark Clouds Gather (2008) by Katy Sara Culling. A brutally honest tale of bipolar disorder leading to a total breakdown, serious anorexia and bulimia, brutal self-harm, 443 suicide attempts but eventual recovery of sorts.

Wasted (1998) by Marya Hornbacher. A brilliantly written autobiography of anorexia and bulimia.

Anorexics on Anorexia (1997) – Rosemary Shelley

www.ingramcontent.com/pod-product-compliance
Ingram Content Group UK Ltd.
Pitfield, Milton Keynes, MK11 3LW, UK
UKHW041412180426
11947UKWH00007B/74